AFTER THE WAR

FORCE OF CIRCUMSTANCE I

1944-1952

THE
AUTOBIOGRAPHY OF

Simone de Beauvoir

AFTER THE WAR
FORCE OF CIRCUMSTANCE, I

1944-1952

With a New Introduction by
TORIL MOI

Translated From the French by
RICHARD HOWARD

PARAGON HOUSE
NEW YORK

First Paragon House edition, 1992

Published in the United States by

Paragon House
90 Fifth Avenue
New York, New York 10011

Manufactured in the United States of America

Library of Congress Cataloging-in-Publication Data

Beauvoir, Simone de, 1908–1986
    [Force des choses. English]
    After the War: Force of circumstance, Vol. I: the autobiography of
Simone de Beauvoir / translated by Peter Green ; introduction by
Toril Moi.—1st Paragon House ed.
        p.   cm.
    Translation of: La force des choses.
    English translation originally published: Putnam, ©1963. With new
introd.
    Contents: v. 1. After the war—
    ISBN 1-55778-523-6 (v. 1)
    1. Beauvoir, Simone de, 1908–1986—Biography.   2. Authors,
French—20th century—Biography.   3. Feminists—France—Biography.
I. Title.
PQ2603.E362Z46713   1992
848'.91409—dc20
[B]   92-15064
                                                                CIP

FOREWORD

I have explained why, after Memoirs of a Dutiful Daughter, *I decided to continue my autobiography. I stopped, breathless, when I had reached the liberation of Paris. I needed to know whether my undertaking was of interest to others. It appears to have been so; yet before resuming, I hesitated once again. Friends, readers, urged me on: "And then? What happened next? Where are you now? Finish up; you owe us the rest. . . ." But from others as well as from myself, there was no lack of objections: "It's too soon. You don't have a sufficient body of work behind you. . . ." Or else: "Wait until you can say everything: lacunae, silences, distort the truth." And also: "You lack perspective." And even: "After all, you reveal more of yourself in your novels." None of this is untrue; but I have no choice. Serene or sour, the indifference of decrepitude would keep me from grasping my subject: that moment when, hard upon a still-vibrant past, the decline sets in. I wanted my blood to circulate in this narrative; I wanted to fling myself into it, still very much alive— to put myself in question before all questions are silenced. Perhaps it is too soon; but tomorrow it certainly will be too late.*

"Everyone knows your story," I've also been told, "it's become public property since '44." But such publicity has been merely one dimension of my private life, and since one of my purposes is to clear up certain misunderstandings, it seems to me worthwhile to tell the whole truth about that life. Involved much more than hitherto with political events, I shall have more to say about them. My narrative, however, will not become more impersonal on that account. If politics is the art of "foreseeing the present," not being a specialist it is an unforeseen present that I shall discuss: the way in which history

has happened to me day by day is an adventure quite as individual as my subjective development.

In the period of which I shall speak, the point was no longer to educate but to fulfill myself; though faces, books, films and encounters mattered to me as a whole, almost none of them was essential to me in itself. When I evoke them, it is often the caprices of memory that control my choice, which does not necessarily imply a value judgment. On the other hand, I shall not linger here over the experiences which I have described elsewhere—my trips to the United States and to China—whereas I shall discuss in detail my visit to Brazil. Of course this will distort the symmetry of my book: so be it. In any case, I make no claim to its being—any more than its predecessor—a work of art. *The term suggests a statue dying of boredom in some villa garden; it is a collector's term, a consumer's term, not a creator's. I should never think of saying that Rabelais, Montaigne, Saint-Simon or Rousseau produced* works of art, *and it is of little concern to me if such a label is denied to my memoirs. No; not a work of art, but my life with its enthusiasms and disappointments, its convulsions, my life attempting to express itself and not to serve as a pretext for elegance.*

This time, too, I shall cut as little as possible. It always amazes me that a memorialist should be criticized for his longueurs. *If he interests me, I'll read him volume after volume; if he bores me, ten pages is already too much. I do not mention the color of the sky, the taste of a fruit out of self-indulgence; telling someone else's life, I would note these so-called trivial details in the same abundance, if I knew them. Not only do they allow us to apprehend a period and a person in flesh and blood, but by their non-significance they are the very touch of truth in a true story. They indicate nothing other than themselves, and the only reason to include them is that they were there: that is enough.*

Despite my diffidences which also apply to this last volume—it is impossible to tell everything—certain critics have accused me of indiscretion. It is not I who began; I prefer rummaging through my past to leaving the task to others.

It has generally been granted that the previous volumes possess one virtue I had striven for: a sincerity as far from boastfulness as from masochism. I hope I have kept it. For over thirty years I have practiced it in my conversations with Sartre, observing myself from day to day with neither shame nor vanity, as I observe the things around me. It is natural to me, not by a special grace, but because of the way in which I consider people, including myself. I believe in our freedom, our responsibility, but whatever their importance, this dimension of our existence eludes description. What can be described is merely our conditioning; I seem to my own eyes an object, a result, without involving the notions of merit or fault in this estimate. If, in the course of time, an action should seem more or less praiseworthy or regrettable, I am much more concerned, in either case, to understand than to judge it. I prefer to fathom rather than to flatter myself, for my love of truth far exceeds my concern for my own image: that love is explained by my own history, and I take no credit for it. In short, because I offer no judgment of myself, I feel no resistance to speaking frankly about my life and myself, at least insofar as I place myself within my own universe. Perhaps my image projected in a different world—that of the psychoanalysts—might disconcert or embarrass me. But so long as it is I who paint my own portrait, nothing daunts me.

My "impartiality" of course must be understood. A Communist, a Gaullist, would describe these years differently; so would a laborer, a farmer, a colonel, a musician. But my opinions, convictions, perspectives, interests, commitments, are stated; they constitute part of the testimony that I offer on their grounds. I am objective to the degree, in other words, that my objectivity envelops me.

Like its predecessor, this book asks the reader for his collaboration. I present, in order, each moment of my development, and the reader must have the patience not to close the accounts before the end. He is not entitled, for instance, to conclude, as one critic has done, that Sartre likes Guido Reni because he liked him when he was nineteen. Indeed, only malice dictates such blunders, and against malice I do not intend to be on my guard. On the contrary, this book contains everything likely to provoke it, and I should be disappointed if it failed to displease someone. I should also be disappointed if it pleased no one, and that is why I suggest that its truth is not expressed in any one of its pages but only in their totality.

Readers have pointed out many small errors and two or three serious ones in The Prime of Life; for all my care, I have certainly made a number of mistakes in this book, too. But I repeat that I have never intentionally distorted the truth.

INTRODUCTION

Picking up the thread from The Prime of Life, *in this volume of her autobiography Simone de Beauvoir tells the story of her life in the postwar years, from the liberation of France in August 1944 to the summer of 1952. This was the period when existentialism became a fashionable phenomenon, inspiring everything from films and nightclubs to hair styles and clothes (long hair and black sweaters). Sartre and Beauvoir became household names, not only in France but all over the Western world. Together they launched* Les temps modernes, *an intellectual magazine that immediately became the focus of literary and political attention on the Left Bank. Publishing essays and novels in rapid succession, Beauvoir was astonishingly productive. Two of her texts from this period, the novel* The Blood of Others (1945) *and* The Second Sex (1949), *became best-sellers. While her next novel* All Men are Mortal (1946) *was a relative failure with critics and readers alike, and her play* Who Shall Die? *failed in the theatre (1945), her travel book* America Day by Day (1948) *was well received in France, and the veritable scandal produced by* The Second Sex *hardly detracted from its impact. The Vatican even put it on the Index. By the time she was forty-two, in 1950, Simone de Beauvoir's reputation as the leading intellectual woman in France was firmly established.*

On the surface of it, then, one might expect Beauvoir to represent this period of her life as a glorious success story. In fact, however, hers is a narrative marked by political and private pain and conflict. In the period from 1944 to 1952, the jubilant hopes of the liberation turned to ashes: by 1947 the dream of a new, united and socialist France, undivided by prewar class politics, shared by the overwhelming majority of French intellectuals in 1944, was in ruins. Instead of forming a broad united front, French political life quickly split into three warring blocs, ranging from the Gaullists on the right, through the various

Christian democrat, liberal or self-styled "radical" parties at the center, to the socialists and the communists on the left.

In this political picture, Beauvoir's voice was that of a left-wing intellectual, deeply critical of the bourgeoisie in her own country, and firmly committed to the socialist ideal of a just, classless society without exploitation, oppression, violence and hunger. She was not, however, a communist, and kept a firm distance between herself and the PCF (the French Communist Party). Her main objection to communist policies, in France as elsewhere, was the authoritarianism and disregard for human rights displayed by Stalinism. As a writer Beauvoir was particularly concerned with freedom of speech: she had no intention of joining a party that imposed censorship on its intellectuals.

*Her distaste for the totalitarianism of communism found its counterpart in her scathing condemnation of the exploitative colonialism of the Western world. For throughout this period French forces, with increasing U.S. material assistance, were fighting to uphold French colonial dominance in Vietnam. As early as May 1945, after a nationalist riot in the Algerian town of Sétif in which 29 Europeans died, French troops massacred between 6,000 and 8,000 Algerian Muslims. In 1947 an uprising in Madagascar left 550 Europeans and 1900 natives dead. In April 1948 a French expeditionary force proceeded to ruthless retaliation: according to official figures 89,000 Madagascans were killed. No wonder Beauvoir felt compelled to question whether such policies truly served the cause of democracy. In fact, at this time in France—and this was greatly to its credit—*Les temps modernes *was the only journal to consistently publish critical reports on colonial conflicts. Caught up in the propaganda war between the superpowers, the rest of the French media paid little or no attention to colonial questions before the Algerian War of Independence (1954–62) finally forced the question to the top of the French political agenda.*

One of the most fascinating aspects of this volume of Beauvoir's memoirs is her evocation of the material and ideological atmosphere of the late 1940s. In the 1990s, at a time when the Berlin Wall has fallen and the Soviet Union exists no more, it is easy to forget the climate of fear that dominated the Cold War. In France the late 1940s were a time of unusual political intensity. The Nazi occupation was only just over, and the French were still reeling from the shock of Hiroshima and the Holocaust, when the fear of a Soviet invasion gripped the nation for the first time in 1947. In 1949 the Soviet Union became an atomic power, and from then on the nuclear threat weighed heavily on Europe. In the summer of 1950, after the outbreak of the Korean War, a Soviet occupation of France was considered imminent. The French were overcome by panic: a whole school class swore a solemn suicide pact that would be effective in the event of a Soviet occupation. "The day the Russians march into Paris, I shall kill myself and my two children," Francine Camus declared. Sartre and Beauvoir themselves quite seriously envisaged having to choose suicide or exile in the immediate future.

Beauvoir's account of her travels to countries untouched by the devastations of war and occupation—Spain, Portugal, Sweden, Switzerland and, above all, the United States—brings out the intolerable poverty of the French. Her pleasure in a Portuguese wool sweater, a pair of Swiss leather shoes or an American coat neatly encapsulates the economic situation in France at the time. The woman who was writing The Second Sex was poorly dressed, badly nourished, and lived in squalid hotel rooms on the Left Bank. Hoping to improve her working conditions, in October 1948 Beauvoir moved to a leaky room in a rundown building near Notre Dame. Yet her own and Sartre's increasing fame guaranteed them an income far beyond that of an ordinary member of the intelligentsia at the time: in France Beauvoir was privileged indeed, in more fortunate countries she was made to feel like the shabby foreigner she was.

In Beauvoir's life, the dismal political situation was doubled by difficult personal circumstances. In January 1945 Sartre left for an extended tour of the United States. In New York he met Dolorès Vanetti ("M." in the text), a charming Frenchwoman with whom he fell passionately in love. By December of that year he was back in New York, and as Beauvoir set out for a short trip to Tunisia early in 1946, she was more worried than she liked to admit. Staying alone in a hotel in the desert she ran out of books to read, and suddenly loneliness closed in on her: "there were moments when it seemed that time had ceased to exist, and I felt a strange weakness come over me," she notes. At those moments she took herself off on long walks in the desert and felt better: "After years of living with others, this encounter with myself stirred me so deeply that I believed it to be the dawn of some sort of wisdom," she writes. Deriving comfort from her new-found capacity to sustain loneliness, she managed not to think too much about Dolorès.

When Sartre returned from the United States in the spring of 1946, he couldn't stop talking about Vanetti: "At present, their attachment was mutual," Beauvoir writes, "and they envisaged spending three or four months together every year." This didn't worry her unduly: "separations held no terror for me," she comments. What really disturbed her, however, is the way in which Sartre insisted on the fact that "[Dolorès] shared completely all his reactions, his emotions, his irritations, his desires." As readers of The Prime of Life will have noticed, Beauvoir's most cherished image of her relationship with Sartre is that of their total unity. According to Beauvoir, they bear the mark of twinship on their brows; as a couple Sartre and herself are truly one: "In more than thirty years, we have only once gone to sleep at night disunited," she claims at the end of the second volume of The Force of Circumstance.

The very thought of another woman sharing a deeper unity with Sartre than

xii   INTRODUCTION

herself is intolerable to Beauvoir. Ruminating over Sartre's account of Dolorès, she experiences even greater anguish than in the traumatic times of the trio (see The Prime of Life*): "Perhaps this indicated a harmony between them at a depth—at the very source of life, at the wellspring where its very rhythm is established—at which Sartre and I did not meet," she worries, "and perhaps that harmony was more important to him than our understanding." It is because of her fear of no longer being* one *with Sartre, that Beauvoir finds herself asking the classical question, echoed by the jilted wife in Beauvoir's own short story* The Woman Destroyed *(1968): "Frankly, who means the most to you, [Dolorès] or me?" Sartre's reply is a masterpiece of ambiguity: "[Dolorès] means an enormous amount to me, but I am with you," he says. Taking him to mean that he loves Dolorès and only stays with herself out of a sense of duty, Beauvoir almost falls apart. Sartre soon manages to put a more soothing gloss on the statement, but Beauvoir's confidence in herself and her relationship with Sartre remained shaken.*

Perhaps that is why she threw herself so wholeheartedly into a relationship with Nelson Algren, the Chicago novelist, during her own trip to the United States in 1947. According to Deirdre Bair's biography, Beauvoir always claimed that Nelson Algren was the "only truly passionate love in my life." With him, she experienced a sexual pleasure she had never known with Sartre— or any other lover, for that matter; in a matter of days she was head over heels in love. Their letters from this period amply demonstrate that the attraction was mutual: if Algren was Beauvoir's "Chicago husband," she was his "Frog wife." Readers curious for more information about this relationship, should read Beauvoir's novel The Mandarins *(1954), in which the liaison between Anne and Lewis closely mirrors that of Beauvoir and Algren.*

Discussing her transatlantic affair with Algren, Beauvoir tends to cast the latter as the victim of her own and Sartre's unbreakable pact: "for although my understanding with Sartre has lasted for more than thirty years," she writes in 1963, "it has not done so without some losses and upsets in which the 'others' always suffered." Neatly glossing over her own pain, this version of events leaves something to be desired. For while there is no doubt that both Vanetti and Algren were deeply hurt in their liaisons with Sartre and Beauvoir, on the evidence of her own text, Beauvoir herself suffered grievously from both affairs. On her return from the United States in 1947, Beauvoir found that Vanetti was still in Paris, and, moreover, that she absolutely refused to leave. Fleeing to the suburbs, Beauvoir abandoned Paris to her rival and hardly set foot in the city for two months. Longing for Algren, suffering from Sartre's obsession with Vanetti, she took drugs for the first and only time in her life, and writes of "two painful months," an "anxiety that bordered on mental aberration," a distress "accom-

panied by a physical panic that my greatest fits of despair, even when enhanced by alcohol, had never produced." "Suddenly I was becoming a stone," she continues, "and the steel was splitting it: that is hell." When Sartre finally put Vanetti back on the boat to New York, the latter complained bitterly of his violence toward her. Dragging themselves through a trip to Scandinavia, Sartre and Beauvoir were distraught with depression and doubt: "I wondered in terror if we had become strangers to one another," Beauvoir writes.

    But the pain of 1947 was just the beginning. Resuming her affair with Algren in 1948, Beauvoir cut her stay on the American continent short because of Sartre. At the cost of much anguish, she returned to Paris only to find that Vanetti had turned up, too. Instead of staying with Beauvoir, Sartre left her in Paris and took off on a holiday with Vanetti. Beauvoir's feelings at this turn of events can easily be imagined. While Sartre's affair with Vanetti took a turn for the worse in 1949, and was finally broken off in 1950, Beauvoir's feelings for Algren took a long time to cool. It was not only the dismal political situation that made 1950 and 1951 "a melancolical year" for Beauvoir. The following year was no better: "one of the darkest periods of my life," she sighs. Her account of their last summer in the United States in 1951 is painful reading indeed. Back in Paris in the autumn of 1951, Beauvoir feels lonely, depressed and unloved. At the age of forty-three she tells herself that her sex life is over: "I'll never sleep again warmed by another's body. . . . When I fully grasped these facts, I felt myself sinking into death. . . . It was like some brutal but inexplicable amputation." The fruits of fame turned out to be bitter rather than sweet: recognized in the streets, Sartre and Beauvoir can no longer live a normal social life. Old friends disappear, and new friendships are hard to find. "As always, Sartre was a great help to me," Beauvoir claims—rather unconvincingly, it must be said. "Yet," she continues—on a more realistic note this time—because of his fame "he seemed further away from me than ever before. . . . I had the feeling that he had been stolen from me."

    Politically disillusioned, aching from the loss of Algren, distanced from Sartre, unhappy with her everyday life in Paris, Beauvoir took refuge in work. In the dark years from 1950 to 1952 she drafted and redrafted a massive new novel, The Mandarins *(published in 1954). Instead of ending this volume of her memoirs on a note of personal sadness, she ends it with a detailed discussion of her own fictional text. There are good reasons for this:* The Mandarins *is, to a great extent, the fictional reworking of her own experiences in the period covered by this volume of* The Force of Circumstance. *Into this novel Simone de Beauvoir pours all her longings and all her losses, as well as her own acute analysis of the political development of the postwar period: it is no exaggeration to say that* The Mandarins *is the* War and Peace *of the Cold War.*

In 1960 Nelson Algren and Simone de Beauvoir met again, and spent the summer together. According to Beauvoir, it was an unproblematic and easy time for both of them. After that, they kept in touch. The first publication of The Force of Circumstance *in English in 1965, however, so infuriated Algren that he vented his rage in spiteful interviews and reviews across the United States. In December 1964, Algren accused Beauvoir in* Newsweek *of "fantasizing a relationship in the manner of a middle-aged spinster. . . . She ain't Heloise and I ain't Abelard—I hope. It's just shopgirl writing—madame Yackety-Yack is not even as good as Ann Landers." And in a review of* The Force of Circumstance *in* Harper's Magazine, *Algren's rage at being cast as secondary in relation to Sartre is evident: Beauvoir is castrating, dishonest and incapable of understanding love: "Anybody who can experience love contingently has a mind that has recently snapped. How can love be* contingent? Contingent upon *what?" he snarls. "Will she ever quit talking?" Algren never spoke or wrote to Beauvoir again. Yet she remained faithful to her experience of their affair: in 1986 she was buried with his ring on her finger.*

Many women have taken Simone de Beauvoir to task for not living up to the splendid feminist principles of The Second Sex. *Why is she so subservient to Sartre? Why does she put up with such unreasonable behavior in her lovers? Why doesn't she throw them out? Why is she so eager to put a good face on everything? Why won't she admit that she has problems? In relation to such questions, her relationship to Algren is no less puzzling than most of her other liaisons. By all accounts, Algren was hardly an easy man to deal with. His biographer, Bettina Drew, admits that he was rather sexist, often treating women as no more than casual objects of desire. Speaking to Deirdre Bair, Beauvoir herself describes him as "unstable, moody, even neurotic." Yet, she adds, "I liked being the only one who understood him." In this casual reply the theme of the fundamental unity with the loved one surfaces again: nobody understands Sartre as well as she does ("we might almost be said to think in common," she writes in 1963), and nobody is closer to Algren, either. Beauvoir's notion of passion is dominated by a longing for merger with the beloved. As long as that deep sense of symbiosis is there, it doesn't occur to her to object to even the most unpleasant or egocentric behavior of her lovers. If they are one, how can she object to their obsessions? What is the difference between their needs and her own? And how can she possibly admit that she is unhappy without provoking instant dissolution of the fundamental union? Sartre's mistresses and Algren's moody silences or sudden rages do not matter in the least: what matters is that deep sense of connection that Beauvoir cherishes more than anything. When that feeling is threatened, whether by Dolorès or Sartre's increasing fame, Beauvoir suffers much pain: depression and loneliness close in on*

*her, leaving her defenseless against a profound sense of desolation and aban-
donment. No wonder she was so surprised at being able to snatch a few moments
of solitary wisdom in the Tunisian desert. In Simone de Beauvoir's life, sadly
enough, those moments were the exception, not the rule.*

*Beauvoir's particular psychological investment in close, symbiotic relation-
ships is not unusual in women. The potentially destructive effects of such
investments have been copiously documented. Simone de Beauvoir's outstand-
ing achievement is to have left us an admirable record of her unceasing struggle
against the destructive aspects of her own psychological needs. It was not easy for
her to turn down Sartre's offer of marriage and set out for a year on her own in
Marseille (see* The Prime of Life*), and she had to fight hard to overcome the
anguish of giving up Nelson Algren. Her persistent and patient efforts to
become an independent woman, to build a literary career for herself, and to
devote herself to the solitary task of writing bear witness to the success of her
struggle. One could hardly expect her to have done it all without displaying the
slightest trace of pain or psychological conflict. Many have wanted to mytholo-
gize Beauvoir. Yet she, like the rest of us, was torn by the contradictions of a
patriarchal society. Reading her autobiography, I am struck at once by her
strength, energy and vitality, and by her helplessness and fragility. When I
realize how hard it was for her to gain a sense of autonomy and independence, I
find her achievements all the more admirable. We don't need to be perfect,
Simone de Beauvoir teaches us, we simply need never to give up. To me, that is
both a comforting and an utterly daunting prospect.*

Toril Moi

AFTER THE WAR

FORCE OF CIRCUMSTANCE, I

1944-1952

CHAPTER I

WE WERE LIBERATED. IN THE streets, the children were singing:

Nous ne les reverrons plus
C'est fini, ils sont foutus.

And I kept saying to myself: It's all over, it's all over. It's all over: everything's beginning. Patrick Walberg, the Leirises' American friend, took us for a jeep ride through the suburbs; it was the first time in years that I'd been out in a car. Once again I wandered after midnight in the mild September air. The bistros closed early, but when we left the terrace of the Rhumerie or the smoky little red inferno of the Montana, we had the sidewalks, the benches, the streets. There were still snipers on the roofs, and my heart would grow heavy when I sensed the vigilant hatred overhead. One night, we heard sirens. An airplane, whose nationality we never discovered, was flying over Paris; V-1s fell on the suburbs and blew houses to bits. Walberg, usually well-informed, said that the Germans were putting the finishing touches to new and even more terrifying secret weapons. Fear returned, and found its place still warm. But joy quickly swept it away. With our friends, talking, drinking, strolling, laughing, night and day we celebrated our deliverance. And all the others who were celebrating too, near or far, became our friends. An orgy of brotherhood! The shadows that had immured France exploded. The tall soldiers, dressed in khaki and chewing their gum, were living proof that you could cross the seas again. They ambled past, and often they stumbled. Singing and whistling, they stumbled along the sidewalks and the subway platforms; stumbling, they danced at night in the bistros and laughed their loud laughs, showing teeth white as children's. Genet, who had had no sympathy with the Germans but who detested idylls, declared loudly on the terrace of the Rhumerie that these costumed civilians had no style. Stiff in their black-and-green carapaces, the occupiers had been something else! For me, these carefree young Americans were freedom incarnate: our own and also the freedom that was about to spread—we had no doubts on this score—throughout the world. Once Hitler and Mussolini had been overthrown and Franco and Salazar driven out, Europe would be cleansed of Fascism for good. Through the C.N.R. charter, France was taking the path of socialism. We believed that the country had been shaken deeply enough to permit a radical remodeling of its structure without new convulsions. *Combat* expressed our hopes by displaying as its motto: *From Resistance to Revolution.*

This victory was to efface our old defeats, it was ours, and the future it opened up was ours, too. The men now in power had been in the Resistance and, to a greater or lesser extent, we knew them all. We could count many of the important figures in the press and the radio as close friends. Politics had become a family matter, and we expected to have a hand in it. *"Politics is no longer dissociated from individuals,"* Camus wrote in *Combat* at the beginning of September, *"it is man's direct address to other men."* We were writers, and that was our job, to address ourselves to other men. Before the war, few intellectuals had tried to understand their epoch; all—or almost all—had failed in the attempt, and the one we had admired the most, Alain, had fallen into disgrace. It was our turn to carry the torch.

I knew then that my destiny was bound to that of all other people; freedom, oppression, the happiness and misery of men was a matter of intimate concern to me. But I have already said that I had no philosophical ambition. Sartre, in *Being and Nothingness,* had sketched a total description of existence whose value depended on his own situation, and he intended to continue this work. He would have to establish his position not only through theoretical speculations, but also by practical choices. Hence he found himself committed to action in a much more radical way than myself. We always discussed his attitudes together, and sometimes I influenced him. But it was through him that these problems, in all their urgency and all their subtlety, presented themselves to me. In this realm, I must talk about him in order to talk about us.

In our youth, we had felt close to the Communist Party insofar as its negativism agreed with our anarchism. We wanted the defeat of capitalism, but not the accession of a socialist society which, we thought, would have deprived us of our liberty. It was in this sense that Sartre wrote in his notebook, on September 14, 1939: *"I am now cured of socialism, if I needed to be cured of it."* Yet in '41, when he was forming a Resistance group, the two words he brought together for its baptism were: socialism and liberty. The war had effected a decisive conversion.

First of all, it had shown him his own historicity; and the shock of this discovery made him realize how much he had been attached to the established order, even while he was condemning it. There is a conservative in every adventurer. To create his image, to project his legend into the future, the adventurer needs a stable society. Utterly dedicated to the adventure of writing, having longed to *be* a great writer, having coveted *la gloire immortelle* since childhood, Sartre had been counting on a posterity that would continue to use the heritage of this century for its own purposes without any break in continuity. At heart, he remained faithful to the same "esthetic of opposition" he had believed in at twenty. Relentless in his denunciation of this society's faults, he still had no desire to overthrow it. Suddenly everything fell apart; eternity exploded into a thousand pieces; he found himself drifting aimlessly between a past of illusions and a future of shadows. He defended himself with his morality of *authenticity:* from the point of view of freedom, all situations could be salvaged if one accepted (assumed) them as a project. This solution was still very close to Stoicism, since circumstances often leave us no other way of transcending ourselves than submission. Sartre, who hated all the little deceptions we practice upon ourselves, could not be satisfied for long by disguising his passivity with verbal protest. He realized that, living not in the absolute but in the transitory, he had to renounce *being* and resolve to *do*. This transition was made easier for him by his previous development. As a thinker, a writer, his primary concern had always been to grasp meanings. But after Heidegger and Saint-Exupéry, whom he read in 1940, had convinced him that meanings came into the world only by the activity of man, practice superseded contemplation. He had said to me during the "phony war"—he had even written as much in a letter to Brice Parrain—that once peace was restored he would go into politics.

His experience as a prisoner left a profound mark on him. It

taught him the meaning of solidarity; far from feeling persecuted, he
took great joy in this participation in a communal life. He loathed
privileges; his pride compelled him to make his way in the world by
his own resources. As merely one cipher among the rest, he took an
immense satisfaction in making a success out of all his undertakings,
starting from scratch. He made friends, imposed his ideas, organized
activities and mobilized the whole camp, at Christmas, to put on and
applaud a play he had written against the Germans, *Bariona*. The
difficulties and the warmth of prison *camaraderie* loosened the contradictions in his anti-humanism. Actually, he was in rebellion against
bourgeois humanism, which reveres a Nature expressed in man; but
if man is still to be created, no task could have impassioned him
more. Henceforth, instead of setting individualism in opposition to
collectivity, he conceived of them only as linked to each other. He
would achieve his freedom not by subjectively accepting the given
situation, but by modifying it objectively, by constructing a future
in accord with his aspirations. This future, in the very name of the
democratic principles to which he was attached, was socialism, from
which he had hitherto been diverted only by his fear of losing his
individuality; but now he saw it both as humanity's only chance and
as a necessary condition of his own fulfillment.

The failure of "Socialism and Liberty" gave Sartre a lesson in
realism; his first serious work came only later, within the F.N. in
collaboration with the Communists.

In '41, as I have said,[1] the Communists turned a cold shoulder to
the *petit-bourgeois* intellectuals and had started a rumor that Sartre
had bought his release by acting as an informer for the Germans. In
'43 they wanted unity of action. There was, in fact, a pamphlet,
reputedly of Communist origin and printed in the South of France,
in which Sartre's name appeared on a blacklist between Château-
briant and Montherlant; he showed it to Claude Morgan, who exclaimed: "That's disgraceful!" and they buried the incident. Sartre's
relations with the Communist resistants had been perfectly friendly.
Now that the Germans were gone, he had every intention of maintaining this accord. Rightist ideologists have explained his alliance
with the Communist Party by psychoanalytical jargon; they have
imputed it to inferiority or rejection complexes, to repressed aggres-
sion, to infantilism and to nostalgia for a church. What nonsense!
The masses were behind the Communist Party; socialism could tri-

1 In *The Prime of Life.*

umph only through the Party. Furthermore Sartre was now aware that his connection with the proletariat entailed a radical reconsideration of his whole existence. He had always supposed the proletariat to be the universal class. But as long as he believed he could attain the absolute by literary creation, his relation to others (*être pour autrui*) had remained of secondary importance. With his historicity he had discovered his dependence; no more eternity, no more absolute. The universality to which, as a bourgeois intellectual, he aspired could now be bestowed on him only by the men who incarnated it on earth. He was already thinking what he later expressed[1]: the true perspective is that of the most disinherited; the hangman can remain ignorant of what he does; the victim experiences his suffering and his death irrecusably; the truth of oppression is the oppressed. It was through the eyes of the exploited that Sartre was to learn what he was. If they rejected him, he would find himself imprisoned in his *petit-bourgeois* individualism.

There were no reservations in our friendship for the U.S.S.R.; the sacrifices of the Russian people had proved that its leaders embodied its true wishes. It was therefore easy, on every level, to co-operate with the Communist Party. Sartre did not contemplate becoming a member. For one thing he was too independent; but above all, there were serious ideological divergences between him and the Marxists. The Marxist dialectic, as he understood it then, suppressed him as an individual; he believed in the phenomenological intuition which affords objects immediately "in flesh and blood." Although he adhered to the idea of *praxis,* he had not given up his old, persisting project of writing an *ethics.* He still aspired to *being;* to live morally was, according to him, to attain an absolutely meaningful mode of existence. He did not wish to abandon—and indeed, never has abandoned—the concepts of negativity, of interiority, of existence and of freedom elaborated in *Being and Nothingness.* In opposition to the brand of Marxism professed by the Communist Party, he was determined to preserve man's human dimension. He hoped that the Communists would grant existence to the values of humanism; and he was to try, with the tools they lent him, to tear humanism from the clutches of the bourgeoisie. Apprehending Marxism from the viewpoint of bourgeois culture, he was to place the latter, by an inverse process, in a Marxist perspective. "Coming from the middle classes, we tried to bridge the gap between the in-

1 In 1952, in *Les Communistes et la Paix.*

tellectual petite bourgeoisie and the Communist intellectuals."[1] On the political level, he felt that its sympathizers should play a role outside of the Communist Party similar to that assumed inside other parties by the Opposition: a role that combined support and criticism.

These pleasant dreams were engendered by the Resistance, which had revealed history to us but had also concealed the class struggle. It seemed that all reactionary influences had been politically liquidated along with Nazism; only that fraction of the bourgeoisie which had cooperated with the Resistance was now participating in public life and accepted the charter of the C.N.R. On their side, the Communists supported the government with "national unanimity." Thorez came back from the U.S.S.R. and told the workers it was their duty to revive our industries, to work, to be patient and to refrain for the time being from all claims. No one spoke of putting back the clock; reformists and revolutionaries were taking the same paths into the future. In this atmosphere, all antagonisms became blurred. That Camus was hostile to the Communists seemed a subjective trait of little importance, since in his struggle to bring the charter of the C.N.R. into effect he was defending exactly the same positions they were. Sartre, a Communist sympathizer, nevertheless approved of *Combat*'s policy enough to write an editorial for it. Gaullists, Communists, Catholics, and Marxists fraternized. All the newspapers expressed the same ideas. Sartre gave an interview to *Carrefour*. Mauriac wrote for *Les Lettres Françaises;* we all sang in chorus our hymn of the future.

Soon *Les Lettres Françaises* began to grow sectarian. *Action* was more open-minded; it seemed possible to reach an understanding with the young men who were running it. Hervé and Courtade even asked Sartre to join them. He refused because *Action* had attacked Malraux in a way we thought unfair. We were very surprised when Francis Ponge, who ran the cultural section, told us that a mountain of articles against Sartre was piling up on his desk. He published some of them, and Sartre replied with a *Mise au Point* (Definition of Terms). He was blamed for being influenced by Heidegger: the political position Heidegger had taken did not retrospectively invalidate all his ideas. Moreover, far from being a quietism or a nihilism, Existentialism was a definition of man through action; if it condemned him to anxiety it did so only insofar as it obliged him to

1 *Merleau-Ponty Vivant.*

accept responsibilities. The hope it denied him was the idle reliance on anything other than himself; it was an appeal to man's will. Sartre was convinced that henceforth the Marxists could no longer consider him an adversary. So many obstacles had been overcome that none now seemed insuperable. From others and from ourselves, we hoped for everything.

Those around us shared in this euphoria. First the family and the old guard of the "fiestas." Then there were the younger members who had joined us. G.-F. Rolland, though he had become a Communist at the age of twenty in the *maquis* and was deeply convinced of the virtues of the Party, tolerated our deviations good-humoredly. Scipion laughed so loudly that we thought he was happy; his specialities were parodies, puns, spoonerisms and picaresque anecdote. Gabriel Astruc, of the great liquid smile, wrote for all the newspapers in strict rotation, and when he wasn't writing he talked—mostly about himself. With touching narcissism, he would make the most naïve and raw admissions about his private life. To be twenty or twenty-five in September of '44 seemed the most fantastic piece of luck: all roads lay open. Journalists, writers, budding film makers, were all arguing, planning, passionately deciding, as if their future depended on no one but themselves. Their gaiety fortified my own. In their company I was their age, though without relinquishing anything of a maturity so dearly come by that I wasn't far from taking it for wisdom; thus I reconciled—in a fleeting illusion—the contradictory privileges of youth and age. It seemed to me that I knew a great deal and that I could do almost anything.

Soon the exiles began to return. Bianca had spent a year hidden in the Vercors with her parents and her husband; she had married one of her classmates. Raymond Aron had left in 1940 for London where he and André Labarthe had edited a review called *La France Libre* which the Gaullists hadn't approved of. Although he wasn't given to effusiveness, when he appeared one morning at the Café de Flore we fell into each other's arms. Albert Palle had reached England somewhat later; parachuted back into France, he had fought in the *maquis*. I found it very moving to see these faces once again; then there were the new ones. Through Camus we met Father Bruckberger, chaplain of the F.F.I., who had just finished making *Les Anges du Péché* with Bresson. He had a *bon vivant* act, and would sit white-robed in the Rhumerie, smoking a pipe, drinking punch and talking lustily. Aron took us to lunch with Corniglion-Molinier who had been condemned to death by Vichy; his furniture had been confiscated, and he was camping out in a vast, luxurious but empty apartment on the Avenue Gabriel; attentive and charming, he was full of stories about the French in London. Romain Gary told us stories, too, one evening on the terrace of the Rhumerie. At a cocktail party given by *Les Lettres Françaises* I caught a glimpse of Elsa Triolet and Aragon. The Communist writer we enjoyed most of all was Ponge; he talked, as he wrote, in little touches, malicious and slightly self-satisfied. At Versailles, during an evening of festivities that included a play by La Fontaine, under the auspices of Éditions de Minuit, I talked for a while with Lise Deharme. I can no longer recall all the hands I shook, all the smiles I exchanged, but I know how much all this sociability pleased me at the time.

These meetings revealed to me a history that was my own but that I had not known before. Aron described the bombing of London in great detail, the cool-headedness of the English, their endurance; the V-1s, which I had watched going over Neuilly-sous-Clermont, red against the black sky, across the Channel were a raucous whistle, an explosion, corpses. "When you heard one, you had to throw yourself flat on the sidewalk," Aron told us. "Once, as I was getting up, I saw a very old lady who had stayed on her feet. She was looking me up and down. I was so annoyed that I reprimanded her: "Madame, in cases like this one should lie down!" He lent me his collection of *La France Libre,* and now I could decipher the war not from the perspective of Paris but from the point of view of London, from the other side. I had been living in a prison; now the world was restored to me.

A ravaged world. Immediately after the Liberation, the Gestapo's torture chambers were discovered; mass graves were unearthed. Bianca told me about the Vercors; she told me about the weeks her father and her husband had spent hidden in a cave; the newspapers gave us the details of massacres, of the executions of hostages; they published accounts of the annihilation of Warsaw. This brutal revelation of the past thrust me back into horror; one's new delight in life gave way to shame at having survived. Some of us were unable to accept. Jausion,[1] sent to the front as a war correspondent by *Franc-Tireur,* did not come back, and his death was almost certainly not

---

[1] His fiancée, as I have said, had been deported. He had been arrested in the Place de la Concorde during the insurrection, then exchanged for a German officer just before the entry of the Allies. He left one novel: *Un Homme Marche dans la Ville.*

accidental. Victory was a costly commodity. In September, the Allied Air Forces turned Le Havre into a rubbish heap; the dead numbered thousands. The Germans dug themselves into Alsace and around Saint-Nazaire. In November, those huge silent engines of destruction, the V-2s, so much more effective than the V-1s, began to fall on London: were they the secret weapons Walberg had talked about, or were there others still to come, even more dreadful? Von Runstedt's army overran Holland and created a famine there. In Belgium, German troops regained a little of the ground they had lost and massacred the inhabitants. In a flash, I saw them re-entering Paris in triumph. And one did not dare to think about what was happening in the concentration camps now that the Germans knew they had lost.

Materially, the situation had grown even worse than the year before; transportation was in chaos; there was a shortage of food, coal, gas and electricity. When it got cold, Sartre wore an old, threadbare lumber jacket. One of his prison camp friends sold me a rabbit coat that kept me warm; but, except for a black suit that I kept for special occasions, I had only the oldest of clothes to put on underneath it, and I continued wearing shoes with wooden soles. Moreover, this didn't matter to me in the least. Ever since I had fallen off my bicycle, I had had a tooth missing; the gap was quite visible, and I didn't even think about having a false one put in: what was the point? In any case, I was old, I was thirty-six; a fact I noted without the slightest bitterness. The flood of events and activities constantly took me out of myself, and I was the least of my worries.

Because of this general poverty, very little was happening in the realm of literature, the arts and the theater. Nevertheless, the organizers of the Salon d'Automne made it into a great cultural manifestation, a retrospective of prewar painting. The canvases had been packed away in the corners of studios and in the dealers' cellars because of the Germans, and it was a great event to see them brought out into the light of day. A whole section was devoted to Picasso; we visited him quite often and knew his recent work, but here all his work of the past few years was gathered together. There were beautiful canvases by Braque, Marquet, Matisse, Dufy, Gromaire, Villon, and the astonishing "Job" of Francis Guber; the surrealists exhibited too: Dominguez, Masson, Miró, Max Ernst. Loyal as ever to the Salon d'Automne, the bourgeoisie arrived in droves, but this time they

were not offered their usual fare; in front of the Picassos, they snick-
ered.

There were not many books coming out; I was bored by Aragon's
Aurélien; and no less by *The Walnut Trees of Altenburg* which had
been published in Switzerland a year before and had prompted old
Groethuysen to remark: "Malraux is in full possession of all his
weaknesses." *L'Arbaléte* published a collection of texts, mostly trans-
lated by Marcel Duhamel, by American authors both unknown—
Henry Miller, Horace McCoy, Nathanael West, Damon Runyon,
Dorothy Baker—and known—Hemingway, Richard Wright, Thomas
Wolfe, Thornton Wilder, Erskine Caldwell, and, of course, Saroyan;
it was impossible to open any periodical without coming across his
name. There was also an English writer in that number: Peter
Cheney. Several new English writers were being mentioned—Auden,
Spender, Graham Greene—but nothing was known about them yet.
Someone lent me Hillary's *The Last Enemy;* shot down over the
Channel, this young pilot, one of the last of the long-haired Oxo-
nians, described with a slightly discordant laugh the operations and
grafts that had restored his eyes, face and hands; by its rejection of all
humanism and all heroism, the story managed to transcend the episode that had inspired it. I also read a great quantity of war books—
of lesser quality—specially printed in the U.S.A. for export; on their
white, red-ruled covers, Liberty brandished her torch. In *A Walk in
the Sun,* Harry Brown told the story of a handful of men landing in
Italy. In *G.I. Joe,* Ernie Pyle drew the portrait of the American
soldier. The Americans adored this "little man in a tattered uniform
who hates war but loves and understands soldiers."[1] He described
the everyday side of war: "The war of the men who wash their
socks in their helmets."[2]

On stage, *No Exit* was revived. Dullin put on *Life Is a Dream.*
The "Spectacle des Alliés" at the Pigalle was mostly a patriotic ceremony; the plays given were of very slight interest. I went to a private
performance of Malraux's film *L'Espoir* which moved me as much as
the book. Except for the Capra series *Why We Are Fighting* and
some old Mack Sennett shorts, the cinema had very little to offer.
Patience! There were fantastic stories of the wonders taking place in
Hollywood. A twenty-seven-year-old genius named Orson Welles had
revolutionized the cinema; he had succeeded in giving the back-

1 Steinbeck.
2 Steinbeck.

grounds of his shots as clear a focus as the foreground, and in his interior shots the ceilings were visible. The technical revolution was so complete, it was said, that we would need special equipment to show the latest American films.

I sent *The Blood of Others* to Gallimard; Sartre gave them *The Age of Reason* and *The Reprieve*. My *Pyrrhus et Cinéas* was published. It was one of the first books to appear after the Liberation; in the general euphoria, and because we had been starved for ideology and literature for four years, this slender essay was very well received. I began to write again. I had all my time to myself because Sartre, who had asked for a leave of absence from the University, was earning money from the cinema and the theater; we had always pooled our resources, we continued to do so, and I was no longer obliged to worry about food. I have so often advised women to be independent and said that independence begins in the purse, that I feel I must explain this attitude which at the time seemed to speak for itself. My material autonomy was assured, since if the need arose I could always go back to my teaching post;[1] it would have seemed stupid and even criminal to sacrifice precious hours in order to prove to myself day by day that I still had this autonomy. I have never directed my actions according to principles but according to ends; I had plenty to do; writing had become a demanding task. It also guaranteed my moral autonomy; in the solitude of risks taken, of decisions to be made, I made my freedom much more real than by accommodating myself to any moneymaking routine. For me, my books were a real fulfillment, and as such they freed me from the necessity to affirm myself in any other way. I therefore devoted myself wholly, and without scruples, to *All Men Are Mortal*. Every morning I went to the Bibliothèque Mazarine to read historical narratives; it was icily cold there, but the story of Charles the Fifth, the episode of the Anabaptists, took me so far from my own body that I forgot to shiver.

The year before, as I have recounted previously, we had conceived two projects: an encyclopedia and a review. Sartre did not pursue the first one, but he held fast to the second. Because of the paper shortage, the only authorized publications were those that had existed before the war and those that had been founded in the free zone during the Occupation. *Esprit, Confluences* and *Poésie 44* were interesting enough, but inadequate to express the age we were living

[1] I had been reinstated at the University, and had taken a leave of absence.

in. We had to find something else. Sartre himself has given an account of his intentions: *"If truth is one, I thought, then we should seek it, as Gide said of God, nowhere except everywhere. Every social product and every attitude—from the most intimate to the most public—are allusive embodiments of it. An anecdote reflects a whole epoch as much as a political constitution does. We would be hunters of meaning, we would tell the truth about the world and about our lives."*[1]

In September, we formed an editorial committee; Camus was too absorbed by *Combat* to be a member; Malraux refused; it was made up of Raymond Aron, Michel Leiris, Merleau-Ponty, Albert Ollivier, Jean Paulhan, Sartre and myself; in those days, none of these names clashed.

We tried to find a title. Leiris, who still retained a taste for scandal from the surrealist days of his youth, proposed a name in that vein: *Grabuge* (Squabble); we didn't use it because, although we certainly wanted to disturb people, we also wanted to be constructive. The title was to convey our positive commitment to the present—so many newspapers had been saying the same things for so many years that there was scarcely anything left to choose between them. We agreed on *Les Temps Modernes;* it was dull, but the reference to the Chaplin film pleased us. (Often, after the magazine had been started, the Argus Agency would send us clippings about the film.) And then, Paulhan pointed out in his mock-serious tone, from which real seriousness was not excluded, it is important to be able to refer to a review by its initials, as in the case of the N.R.F.; and T.M. had a good ring to it. The second problem was the format of the cover. Picasso designed one which was very handsome but really more suitable for an art magazine than for *Les Temps Modernes;* it was impossible to fit a table of contents into it; its partisans on the committee, however, made it the subject of several quarrels that grew quite violent, though without bitterness. In the end, a Gallimard designer submitted a project that reconciled us all. We were discussing no more than trifles, but already I was beginning to enjoy myself enormously; this community of enterprise seemed to me the highest form of friendship. In January, since Sartre was away on a trip, I went in his name to Soustelle, the Minister of Information at that time, to ask him to allot us a quota of paper. Leiris, who knew Soustelle through the *Musée de l'Homme,* went with me. Soustelle was very

[1] *Merleau-Ponty Vivant.*

pleasant but the composition of the editorial committee made him shy away slightly. "Aron? Why Aron?" He complained of his anti-Gaullist attitude. In the end, he made promises which were kept several months later.

As soon as the trains began running again, we went to spend three weeks with Mme Lemaire; sitting in a packed compartment, we rode from eight in the morning till eight at night; the train didn't take the usual route; we left our luggage at the Lion d'Angers and walked the seventeen kilometers from there to La Pouèze without a stop. This stay, like all the others, was happy and without incident.

Back in Paris, I made it my principal task to get my play *Les Bouches Inutiles* performed. Sartre had given a copy to Raymond Rouleau. He told me that I had "not set my sights high enough"; the concision of the dialogue bordered on aridity. I passed the script on to Vitold; he told me he was quite willing to direct it. Badel, the director of the Vieux Colombier, agreed to produce. Vitold began to hold auditions and cast some of the parts; I had always intended the part of Clarice for Olga. It was suggested that Douking should do the sets, and I discussed them with him. All this activity meant that I went to dinner several times at Badel's with Sartre. One evening we played Murder, and I was very proud because I was the only detective who discovered the killer. I grew fond of Gaby Sylvia whose beauty and talent left her unsatisfied and who wanted to educate herself: Robert Kanters was tutoring her quite seriously for the *baccalauréat*. But I didn't really feel at ease in this too-luxurious salon where people did not speak my language. Gaby Sylvia wore gowns by Rochas that dazzled one by their cunning simplicity; next to them, my black suit, the artlessly simple dress I had had made in La Pouéze, seemed almost a discourtesy. I was very sociable in those days, but the ritual of society bored me.

"Would you and Sartre like to meet Hemingway?" Lise asked me one evening. "Of course!" I said. That was the sort of proposal that really pleased me. Though this one didn't surprise me all that much. Lise's principal pastime, since the Liberation, was what she called "Hunt-the-American." The Americans were very free with their cigarettes and their rations, and Lise, always famished, had every intention of profiting from their prodigality. Usually alone, though sometimes, in the beginning, with Scipion, she would take a seat on the terrace of the Café de la Paix or along the Champs-Élysées and wait for a G.I. to speak to her; she never lacked admirers. If she found one who seemed both discreet and entertaining, she would accept a drink, a jeep ride, a dinner; in exchange for the promise of a rendezvous, which she generally failed to keep, she would bring back to the hotel tea, Camels, instant coffee and tins of Spam. The game had its risks. Along the boulevards, soldiers would call out: "Zigzig Blondie"; she would laugh and walk on; if they didn't stop, she would shout insults at them that would make a soldier blush, for her English vocabulary equaled her French in eloquence. One of them, in the Place de l'Opéra, got annoyed; he banged her head against a lamppost and knocked her out. But she had enjoyable encounters too, sometimes. She had made friends with a happy-go-lucky, blond giant who turned out to be Hemingway's younger brother; he used to show her photos of his wife and children, bring her cartons of food and talk to her about the best seller he was going to write. "I know the recipe," he told her.

That evening, Hemingway, who was a war correspondent, had just arrived in Paris and had arranged for his brother to come and see him at the Ritz where he was staying; the brother had suggested that Lise come with him and bring Sartre and myself along. The room, when we went in, bore no resemblance at all to the idea I had always had of the Ritz; it was large but ugly, with its two brass bedsteads; Hemingway was lying on one of them in pajamas, his eyes shielded by a green eyeshade; on a table within easy reach stood a respectable quantity of Scotch, some bottles half empty, others entirely so. He heaved himself up, grabbed hold of Sartre and hugged him. "You're a general!" he said as he squeezed him. "Me, I'm only a captain; you're a general!" (When he'd been drinking he always pushed modesty a bit too far.) Our conversation, punctuated by numerous glasses of Scotch, continued in this enthusiastic vein; despite his flu, Hemingway was bursting with vitality. Sartre, overcome by sleep, tottered away at about three in the morning; I stayed until dawn.

Bost wanted to become a journalist; Camus read the manuscript of the book he had written during the war about his experiences as an infantry private, *Le Dernier des Métiers;* he took an option on it for the series *Espoir* which he was editing for Gallimard and sent Bost to the front as a war correspondent. Whenever you asked Camus for a favor, he would do it so readily that you never hesitated to ask for another; and never in vain. Several of our younger friends also wanted to work for *Combat;* he took them all in. Opening the paper in the morning was almost like opening our mail. Toward the end of

November, the United States wanted its war effort to be better known in France and invited a dozen reporters to the States. I've never seen Sartre so elated as the day Camus offered him the job of representing *Combat*. To obtain all the necessary papers, as well as the dollars, he had to go through a labyrinth of red tape. He made his way through the whole thing during a freezing December with a joy marred only by a nagging uncertainty: in those days nothing was ever definite. And, in fact, there were two or three days when it looked as though the project had fallen through; Sartre's dismay then told me how much he wanted to go.

It meant so many things, America! To begin with, everything inaccessible; its jazz, cinema and literature had nourished our youth, but it had always been a great myth to us as well; myths do not allow themselves to be handled. The trip was to be made by plane; it seemed unbelievable that Lindbergh's great exploit should now be within our reach. America was also the country which had sent our deliverance; it was the future on the march; it was abundance, and infinite horizons; it was a crazy magic lantern of legendary images; the mere thought that they could be seen with one's own eyes set one's head whirling. I rejoiced, not only for Sartre's sake, but also for my own, because I knew that one day I was sure to follow him down this new road.

I had hoped that the New Year celebrations would revive the gaiety of the "fiestas," but on December 24th, the German offensive had only just been halted, and the air was full of anxiety. Bost was at the front, Olga was worried; we spent a little while with Camille and Dullin, but it was dreary there; at about one in the morning, we walked with Olga and a few others to Saint-Germain-des-Prés and finished the night at the beautiful Evelyne Carral's; we ate turkey; Mouloudji sang his usual successes and Marcel Duhamel—who had not yet begun editing the *Série Noire*—sang some American songs with great charm. We celebrated New Year's Eve with Camus who was living in Gide's apartment on the Rue Vaneau; there was a trapeze there and a piano. Directly after the Liberation, Francine Camus had arrived from Algeria, very blond, very fresh-looking, and beautiful in her slate-blue suit; but we hadn't met her often, and several of the guests we didn't know at all. Camus pointed one of them out to us, a man who had scarcely spoken a word all evening. "He's the man I modeled *The Stranger* on," he said. For us, the gathering lacked intimacy. One young woman forced me into a cor-

ner and began accusing me vindictively: "You don't believe in love!"
At about two in the morning, Francine played some Bach. No one
drank very much except Sartre; he was convinced that the party was
just like old times, and he was soon too elated with alcohol to be able
to tell the difference.

He left on January 12th, in a military plane. There was no civil-
ian mail service between the United States and France; the only way
I could get news of him was by reading his articles. He began his
career as a journalist with a *gaffe* that shook Aron to the core: he described the anti-Gaullism of the American leaders during the war
with such satisfaction that he was almost sent straight back to France.

According to an agreement made between Camus and Brisson,
some of the articles were supposed to be given to the latter; Sartre
sent him his impressions, the notes and reflections written in passing,
keeping the pages that had cost him most effort and struggle for
Combat. Camus, having read a sprightly and entertaining description of American cities in *Le Figaro* the day before, was flabbergasted
when he received a careful study of the Tennessee Valley Authority.

Then my chance came. My sister had married Lionel, who was
now attached to the French Institute in Lisbon; he was the editor of
a Franco-Portuguese review called *Affinidades*. He invited me, on
behalf of the Institute, to go to Portugal and give some lectures on
the Occupation. I rushed to the offices of the Relations Culturelles
and demanded a travel permit. I had to ask an enormous number of
people; but they all promised to do what they could, and I was consumed with hope.

At the Vieux Colombier, they began rehearsing the third and
fourth scenes of *Les Bouches Inutiles*. I was getting material together
for *Les Temps Modernes* and making contacts. At the Deux Magots,
I met Cyril Connolly, the editor of the English review *Horizon*
which had published the work of Resistance writers during the war,
among others Aragon's *Crève-Coeur*. He told me about the new English literature and about Koestler, who was living in London. I had
enjoyed *Spanish Testament;* on Christmas night, Camus had lent me
Darkness at Noon and the next night I had read it straight through
without stopping; I was pleased to learn that Koestler enjoyed Sartre's
books. At lunch, at dinner, I kept meeting old friends again; we went
to Chéramy, to the Vieux Paris, to the Armagnac, to the Petit Saint-
Benoît; I spent my evenings with one or another at the Montana, the
Méphisto or the Deux Magots. Bost took me to lunch once at the

Restaurant du Scribe, to which all the war correspondents had *entrée;* it was an American enclave in the heart of Paris: white bread, fresh eggs, jam, sugar, Spam.

I made new friends. Before the war, an unknown woman had sent Sartre a copy of her little book *Tropisms,* which had gone unnoticed and whose quality struck us both; this was Nathalie Sarraute; Sartre had written to her and met her. In '41 she had worked in a Resistance group with Alfred Péron; Sartre had seen her again recently, and I had made her acquaintance. That winter I went out with her a lot. She was the daughter of Russian Jews exiled by the czarist persecutions at the beginning of the century, and it was to these circumstances, I suppose, that she owed her restless subtlety. Her vision of the world spontaneously accorded with Sartre's own ideas: she was hostile to all essentialism, she did not believe in clearly defined characters or emotions, or, indeed, in any ready-made notions. In the book she was writing at the time, *Portrait of a Man Unknown,* she was determined to recapture, beneath its commonplaces, life's ambiguous truth. She was very reticent and talked mostly about literature, but with passion.

During the autumn, through my companion in a cinema queue on the Champs-Élysées, I met a tall, elegant, blond woman with a face both brutally ugly and radiantly alive: Violette Leduc. A few days later, at the Flore, she handed me a manuscript. "Confessions of a woman of the world," I said to myself. I opened the book: "My Mother never gave me her hand." I read the first half of the story without stopping; it fell off suddenly, the end was just padding. I told Violette Leduc this. She scrapped the last chapters and wrote new ones as good as the beginning; not only did she have talent, she knew how to work. I suggested the book to Camus; he accepted it immediately. When *L'Asphyxie* came out, several months later, it did not reach a wide public, but it gained the favor of many discriminating readers and won its author the friendship of Genet and Jouhandeau. Violette Leduc was not, in fact, a *femme du monde* at all; when I knew her, she earned her living by going out to the farms of Normandy, finding meat and butter, and bringing them back in her arms to Paris; she invited me to dinner several times in the black-market restaurants she supplied with food; she was gay and often funny, but she gave the impression that there was something violent and mistrustful lurking beneath her apparent openness; she told me with great pride about her bargaining, her forced marches across the countryside, the village bistros, the trucks, the dark trains; she felt quite naturally on the same footing as the peasants, the truck drivers and the peddlers she dealt with. It was Maurice Sachs, with whom she was very friendly, who had encouraged her to write. She lived in utter solitude. I introduced her to Colette Audry, whom I saw quite often, and also to Nathalie Sarraute; a friendship sprang up between them, but was soon broken off by the clash of their temperaments.

The weeding out of collaborators after the Liberation immediately created divisions among the ex-members of the Resistance; everyone agreed that the way it was done was wrong; but while Mauriac preached forgiveness, the Communists were demanding severity; Camus, in *Combat,* was trying to work out a middle course; Sartre and I shared his point of view: vengeance is useless, but there were certain men who could have no place in the world we were trying to build. Practically speaking, I had little to do with it; I had enrolled in the C.N.E. on principle, but I never so much as showed my face at any of their meetings; I thought that Sartre's presence there made mine superfluous. However, hearing about the decisions of the Committee through Sartre, I quite agreed that its members should not write in reviews and newspapers which accepted material from ex-collaborators. I did not want to hear the voices of people who had consented to the death of millions of Jews and Resistance members; I did not want to find their name in any publication side by side with my own. We had said: "We shall not forget"; I was not forgetting that.

It was a tremendous shock, therefore, when a few days before Brasillach's trial someone—I can't remember who it was—asked me to sign a document Brasillach's lawyers were sending around: the undersigned declared their solidarity as writers with the defendant, and asked the court's indulgence.[1] In no way, on no level, did I feel the slightest solidarity with Brasillach; how many times I had wept with rage as I read his articles! "No mercy for the murderers of our country," he used to write; he had claimed the right "to point out those who betray us" and had used it freely; under his editorship, the staff of *Je Suis Partout* denounced people, specified victims, and urged the Vichy Government to enforce the wearing of the yellow star in the Free Zone. They had done more than accept; they had demanded the death of Feldman, Cavaillès, Politzer, Bourla, the deportation of

[1] I don't recall the exact wording of the petition, but this was its substance.

Yvonne Picard, Péron, Kaan, Desnos. It was with these friends, dead or alive, that I felt solidarity; if I lifted a finger to help Brasillach, then it would have been their right to spit in my face. There was not even a moment's hesitation on my part, the problem did not even arise. Camus had the same reaction. "We have nothing to do with those people," he said to me. "The judges will decide; it's their business, not ours."

Nevertheless, I wanted to watch the trial; my signature carried no weight, my refusal was a mere gesture, but even a gesture commits one to a responsibility, and it seemed too easy to evade mine by mere indifference. I managed to get a seat in the press gallery; it was not a pleasant experience. The reporters casually took notes; they drew little pictures in their notebooks; they yawned; the lawyers declaimed; the judges sat; the presiding magistrate presided; it was a play, a ceremony. For the accused it was the moment of truth in which his life and death were weighed in the balance. Confronted by the futile pomp of the Assizes, he alone, his fate condensed into this moment, existed in flesh and blood. He faced his accusers calmly, and when the sentence fell he did not flinch. In my eyes, this courage effaced nothing; it is the Fascists who attach more importance to how we die than to our acts. Nor did I accept the way in which time had changed my anger into resignation; resignation cannot bring the dead to life, nor wash their murderers clean. But, like so many others, I was troubled by the apparatus of justice which, by transforming this executioner into a victim, gave his condemnation an appearance of inhumanity. As I came out of the Palais de Justice, I met some Communist friends and told them about my distress. "You should have stayed at home then," they replied dryly.

Some days later, Camus confided somewhat sheepishly that, yielding to certain pressures and for reasons that he did not explain very clearly, he had finally signed a petition for a recommendation of clemency. Personally, although on the morning of the execution I could scarcely tear my thoughts away from it, I have never regretted my abstention. People have condemned the weeding out of collaborationists for dealing more severely with those who talked approvingly about the Atlantic Wall than with those who built it. To me, it seems utterly unjust that economic collaboration should have been passed over, but not that Hitler's propagandists in this country should have been so severely dealt with. By trade, by vocation, I attach an enormous importance to words. Simone Weil used to demand that anyone who used writing to tell lies to men should be put on trial, and I understand what she meant. There are words as murderous as gas chambers. Jaurès' assassin was armed with words, words drove Salengro to suicide. In the case of Brasillach, there was no question of a mere "offense of opinion"; his denunciations, his advocacy of murder and genocide constituted a direct collaboration with the Gestapo.

The Germans had lost, but they were desperately hanging on. Famine: they had brought the ancient scourge back to Europe again. Scratching at the earth, gnawing the bark of trees, thousands of the Dutch had struggled in vain against this medieval death. Bost brought back some photos from Holland that Camus showed me. "We can't publish these!" he said, and he spread out on his desk pictures of children without bodies and without faces: nothing but eyes; huge, mad eyes. The newspapers only released the least ghastly, and even those one could scarcely bear to look at.

On the evening of February 27th, I got into the train for Hendaye, armed with escudos and my travel permit; a scrap of paper with red, white and blue stripes, it had, in my eyes, all the glamor of an old parchment scroll with a thick wax seal. My neighbor was studiously reading a life of Stalin. "It's very dry," he said; the whole night, he kept up an exchange of remarks on Bolshevism with two young women; on the whole, he was pro. I finished Peter Cheney's *Poison Ivy;* I began Graham Greene's *Brighton Rock* and toward dawn I fell asleep. Suddenly the sky was blue: Hendaye. Except for myself and a little old man who was also going to Madrid, the end of the line; to cross a frontier was still a rare privilege. I had not done so for six years, and it was fifteen since I had last said good-bye to Spain. I had to wait an hour in the office of the commanding officer. At last the barrier was raised, I saw once more the customs officers' shiny two-cornered caps. By the side of the road, a woman was selling oranges, bananas and chocolate; my throat gagged with desire and revulsion: all this plenty only a few yards away from us, why was it forbidden? Suddenly all the shortages in France no longer seemed inevitable; I had the impression that someone was imposing a penance on us. Who? And with what right? At customs, they changed my escudos and refused my francs. Carrying my suitcase, I walked the mile and a half between the frontier and Irun, reduced to a heap of ruins by the Civil War. On the train I met the old man again. He told me that the Spaniards who had seen me go by along the road had said: "She must be poor; she has no stockings!" And it was true that we were poor: no stockings, no oranges, and our money was worthless. On the station platforms I saw young women sauntering, laughing and chatting, their legs in silk stockings; in the towns we passed through I saw shop windows piled high with food. When we stopped, men walked along the platform selling fruit, sweets, ham; the station buffets were crammed with things to eat. I remembered the station at Nantes, where we were all so hungry and so tired, and where we could find nothing to buy but a few crumbling cookies at an exorbitant price. A furious solidarity with the poverty of France raged inside me.

Then I fell asleep; when I awoke, France was far behind; above the plateaux with their velvety covering of frost spread a sky of triumphant blue. Spain. The Escorial, just as it had been fifteen years before; in other days I had gazed at the age-old stones without surprise; now their permanence disconcerted me; the norm, it seemed to me, was the ruined villages and the ramshackle houses in the suburbs of Madrid.

In Madrid, I could not find my past; the same shadowy cafés were there on the Gran Vía, the same smell of hot oil hung over the Plaza Mayor, but my eyes had changed; the abundance that had been invisible before seemed something quite new to me now and dazzling. Silk, wool, leather, food! I walked till I was out of breath, and as I walked I ate; I sat down and ate—raisins, brioches, *gambas*, olives, pastry, fried eggs, milk chocolate; I drank wine and real coffee. In the crowded streets of old Madrid, in the wealthy neighborhoods, I watched all the passers-by for whom the dramatic history I had just lived through was no more than a rumor. I was stopped short by a display window: superb photographs with captions underneath extolling the heroism of "the women of Germany during the war," the heroism of the *Volksturm;* it was a German propaganda center. I stood there, I saw with my own eyes these pictures of heroic crusaders, members of the S.S. A little later, Madrid streamed with light; I mixed with the crowd that flowed indolently up and down the Alcala, just as it used to; here, the thread of time had been mended, but it was not my time, mine had been broken, forever. Suddenly my mind was filled with anguish; one day, in Rouen, another conscience had taken my place in the center of things; on the Alcala, it was the same shock that harrowed me. Until that moment, the subject of history had been France; now Spain, separate and foreign, was imposing its presence on me with such force that it became the subject instead; France was becoming a misty object on the horizon, and I myself, powerless to affect these places where my body moved, had ceased to exist. There was merely a thick fog of weariness that belonged to no one, dragging itself through the crowd.

Next day I was myself again; but I walked through the Prado like a bored tourist. I was cut off from El Greco, from Goya, from the past, from eternity; my century clung to my feet and hindered my steps; I did not fully return to myself until it had been restored to me, on the bald, battered, cracked hill where the University used to stand. There were people sitting about on this empty lot, children were playing, men were sleeping; all around rose tiers of new apartment houses and factories; in the center, the remains of houses, stretches of wall, doors that led nowhere; in the wrecked villages of Normandy, I had walked among rubbish heaps that were brand-new, but these bricks had the dignity conferred on ruins, since Volney and Horace Vernet, by literature and art; yet their history was engraved in my own life, deep inside me; that, too, was a change. In the old days I walked through a universal time, as though along a road; now it was inside of me, a dimension of my experience; at intervals, stretching into the distance, was the inscription: VIVA FRANCO; red and yellow flags fluttered on all the new apartment buildings. *I was wearing a red and yellow scarf and a man had spat after me: "None of that here!"* I considered the dry plains of Castile stretching out at my feet, and the distant snow-covered mountains, and at last managed to return to reality: 1945, Franco's Spain. There were *falangistas,* policemen and soldiers on every street corner; on the sidewalks, a procession of priests and little children dressed in black went by, carrying crosses. The well-fed bourgeois I passed on the Gran Vía had hoped for a German victory. And the splendor of their avenues was only a façade.

A friend had given me the address of some Spanish people who were anti-Franco. On their advice I went to Tetuán, to Vallecas. Just north of Madrid, I saw, suspended on the hillsides, a district the size of a big town and sordid as a shantytown: hovels with red roofs and rubble walls, filled with naked children, goats and hens; no drains and no water. Young girls passed back and forth, bent beneath the weight of buckets; people walked about barefoot or in slippers, almost naked; occasionally a flock of sheep would cross one of the alleys, raising a cloud of red dust. Vallecas was less rustic, it smelled of factories; but the poverty was the same; the streets were used as garbage dumps; the women washed out their rags on the doorsteps of their huts; they were all dressed in black, their faces so hardened by poverty that they looked almost wicked. A worker earns 9 to 12 pesetas per day, I was told; I looked at what things cost, and I understood why nobody in the markets seemed to smile. These people were getting from a quarter to a half pound of bread a day, and a handful of chick-peas, which cost 5 pesetas a pound on the black market. Eggs and meat were completely beyond the means of people in the suburbs. The big baskets of rolls and fritters I saw women selling on the corners of the main streets were treats only for the rich, like the people I had seen in the railway stations, and they alone profited from the abundance I had envied.

I looked, I listened. I was told how, during the war years, the Falange had collaborated with Germany; the police had been in the hands of the Gestapo; the leaders had attempted to propagate anti-Semitism, but in vain, for the word Jew today awakened no echo among the Spaniards. The people as a whole were growing increasingly impatient under the dictatorship. The week before, three bombs had exploded in the quarters of some *falangistas* and two men had been killed; as a reprisal, Franco had ordered seventeen Communists to be shot; many more were killed without such publicity, and torture was habitual in the prisons. What was keeping the Americans from driving Franco out? I wondered. But I had no doubt that they would decide to do so before long.

In Lisbon, I found my sister and Lionel waiting at the station; in the taxi, walking, standing, sitting, in the street, in the restaurant where we ate, in their apartment, we talked until I was felled by sleep. I described the gaiety of this arrival in *The Mandarins*. Lisbon was like Marseilles, like Athens, like Naples and like Barcelona: a burning city, whipped by the smell of the sea; the past suddenly became alive again in the novelty of its hills and promontories, its soft colors, its white sails.

As in Madrid, the opulence of the stores seemed to me part of another age; I entered it. "What are those clogs you're wearing?" my sister had asked, staring down at my feet; and immediately took on the job of dressing me. Never in my life had I surrendered to such a debauch; my lecture tour was very well paid, and in one afternoon I assembled a complete wardrobe: three pairs of shoes, a bag, stockings, lingerie, sweaters, dresses, skirts, blouses, a white wool jacket, a fur coat. At the cocktail party given by the French Institute I was dressed in all-new clothes. There I met some of Lionel's Portuguese friends, all opposed to the regime; they told me resentfully about Valéry, who had not wanted to see anything in Portugal except the blue sky and the pomegranate trees in bloom. And all that nonsense about the mystery and the melancholy of the Portuguese soul! Out of seven million Portuguese, there are seventy thousand who have enough to eat; the Portuguese are sad because they're hungry.

With my sister and Lionel, I listened to *fados*, I watched a Portuguese bullfight. I walked in the gardens of Cintra, among the camellias and the tree ferns. Despite the "carless days" and the gas rationing, we made a long tour through the Algarve in a car lent by the French Institute; time had not dulled this pleasure: finding new aspects of the world day after day, from hour to hour. I saw earth the color of Africa covered with mimosa, bristling with aloes; I saw steep cliffs breasting an ocean calmed by the soft sky, whitewashed villages, baroque churches statelier than the Spanish ones. Often, behind the sober façade with its curving lines, we found what seemed like a magic cave; the walls and the columns were covered with crude paintings, and the confessionals, the pulpit, the altar as well; from the shadows emerged strange objects made of wood, cloth, hair and wax that turned out to be Christs or Saints. Along the roads, I passed peasants in sheepskin trousers, with many-colored blankets thrown over their shoulders; the women wore brilliant dresses; on top of the kerchiefs knotted below their chins, they set wide sombreros; many balanced a large jar on their heads, or on one hip. From time to time, I noticed groups of men and women bent over the earth, all hoeing together in the same rhythm; red, blue, yellow and orange, their costumes were dazzling in the sunlight. But I no longer allowed myself to be deceived; there was a word whose weight I was beginning to appreciate: hunger. Under their bright clothes, these people were hungry; they went barefoot, with stony faces, and in the false gaiety of the village I could see the dulled look in the men's eyes; under the terrible weight of the sun, they were consumed by a wild fire of despair. The following week, we took the train for Oporto; at every station the train was invaded by beggars. At night, Oporto glittered; in the morning, it was red and beautiful beneath the warm white mist that rose from the Douro; but it did not take me long to discover the damp filth of the "unhealthy sectors" teeming with scrofulous children; little girls in rags were digging avidly into the trash cans. Nevertheless, I did not yield to disgust, or to compassion; I drank *vinho verde* and arbutus brandy, I lost myself in the gaiety of my blood and of the sky; we got up early to see the dawn bleach the sea; we watched the harbor lights appear in the evening, as the ocean slowly consumed the glowing sun; I joyfully accepted the beauty of the landscape and the buildings: the flowered slopes of the Minho, Coimbra, Tomar, Batalha, Leiria, Óbidos. But everywhere the poverty was too flagrant to be forgotten for long. At Braga, it was fiesta; there were processions and a fair; I bought scarves, vases, jugs, pottery roosters; I admired the magnificent lyre-horned oxen, paired in carved wooden yokes; but it was impossible to ignore the beggars, the children covered with scabs, the lines of barefoot peasants, the women bent beneath their burdens. At Nazaré, the prettiness of the little harbor, the boats, the costumes did not mask the sadness in the people's eyes. The Portuguese bourgeoisie bore others' poverty with the utmost serenity. To the pale children who asked them for alms, the ladies in their furs would reply impatiently: "*Tenha paciência.*" At V., a little port of the Minho, we dined on a terrace with the consular agent, a Portuguese; some children silently watched us eating; he chased them away; one of them came back, and I gave him 5 escudos; the Portuguese leaped up. "That's too much! He'll just go buy himself candy!"

During the war, Portugal had offered all its sympathy and a certain amount of help to Germany; now that Hitler had been defeated, the government was attempting a rapprochement with France, and it was in accord with this policy that the French Institute had been authorized to sponsor my lecture tour. I had been a teacher, so talking in public did not frighten me; but there was a gap that often discouraged me between my audiences and the experiences I was trying to evoke; they came to hear me out of idleness, out of snobbery, and often with ill will, for many of them still held Fascism very close to their hearts. At V., the audience was icy; no one wanted to believe in the prison camps, the executions, the tortures; the consular agent said, as I stood up at the end: "Well! I must thank you for having told us about all these things. Up till now we have heard nothing about them, nothing whatever," and he emphasized the last word with an ironic inflection. The Francophiles, on the other hand, turned my reports into epics; I was overcome with shame when I read in one illustrated magazine: "Simone de Beauvoir reports: 'We cooked our potatoes over fires of newspapers; we kept the kerosene to throw at German tanks.' " Paris had suffered both more and less than they imagined; had been both less self-satisfied and less heroic; all the questions they asked me were beside the point.

On the credit side, I was very interested by my talks with the Portuguese anti-Fascists; most of the ones I met were ex-teachers, ex-ministers of state, men of middle age or older; they wore starched collars, bowlers or black derbies, and put their trust in an eternal France and Georges Bidault; but they provided me with a host of documents on the population's standard of living, on the economic organization of the country, on the budget, the unions, the incidence of illiteracy, and also on the police, the prisons and political repression. A young doctor took me into some working-class homes—hovels where the staple diet was stale sardines; he gave me precise figures on the inadequacy of the hospitals, of medical attention and general health measures; although, in fact, one had only to walk through Lisbon and keep one's eyes open to be aware of such things. The people were deliberately kept in a state of filth and ignorance: Fatima was being launched. "The terrible thing is that Salazar will never fall until Franco does," these people told me. And they added that the two dictators would find the defeat of the Axis a very minor inconvenience indeed! The English capitalists had considerable interests in Portugal, America was bargaining for air bases in the Azores; Salazar could count on Anglo-American support; that is why it was so necessary to awaken public opinion in France. One ex-minister asked me to take back a letter to Bidault: if Bidault would help him set up a new government, then that government would cede Angola to France. This colonialist scheme would have upset me considerably if I had taken it seriously, but I knew that the letter would end up in the wastepaper basket. I delivered it to the Quai d'Orsay.

I arrived back in Paris at the beginning of April, on a beautiful sunny day. I had brought fifty kilos of food with me: hams, rust-colored *chorizos,* Algarve cookies sticky with sugar and eggs, tea, coffee, chocolate. Triumphantly I made the rounds of my friends. To the women I gave sweaters and shawls; for Bost, Camus and Vitold I had brought back checkered fishermen's shirts from Nazaré. And I paraded myself in all my new finery. A very elegant woman I did not know came up to me in the Place Saint-Augustin. "Where did you find those?" she asked me, gesturing toward my new crepe-soled shoes. "In Lisbon," I told her, not without pride; it is so difficult not to become vain about one's own good luck. Vitold had some unpleasant news for me; he had quarreled with Badel, who no longer wanted to produce my play; but we should be able to find another theater quite easily, he assured me.

I wrote my articles; the one on Madrid appeared in *Combat-Magazine*, under my name; the Spanish radio accused me of inventing slanders for money without leaving Paris. *Combat* began printing a series of articles on Portugal which I signed with a pseudonym in order not to compromise my brother-in-law; Camus was in North Africa at the time, and Pascal Pia, who was replacing him, abruptly broke off the series; it was continued in *Volontés*, which was edited by Collinet. I received encouraging letters from a certain number of Portuguese, but the country's propaganda service protested. I returned to work on my novel; now, through the windows of the Bibliothèque Mazarine, I could see leaves and blue sky, and I often read the old stories over for the simple pleasure of reading, without thinking of my hero.

Dullin put on *King Lear*. Camille had made a good adaptation, and also helped Dullin with the staging. The costumes and sets—which I personally liked a lot—were a little aggressive in their extravagance; but the cast was good, with a ravishing Cordelia, Ariane Borg; by turns hateful, pathetic, decrepit, visionary, inhuman and only too human, Dullin had managed to make *Lear* one of his best creations. Yet the critics fell on the production with all the savagery at their command. The public stayed away. For Dullin, this flop was a major disaster; there was talk of taking the direction of the Sarah-Bernhardt Theater away from him. He asked me to defend his *Lear*. I wrote an article that Ponge got printed in *Action*. I accused the critics of bad faith: they had attacked the production because they did not dare admit they were bored with Shakespeare. My little polemic was more violent than inspired; I had no great hopes for it, and nothing came of it. It merely earned me a few steadfast enemies.

It was spring, the first spring of peace. They were showing Prévert's *Les Enfants du Paradis* in Paris, and at last some American films: *I Married a Witch, My Girl Friday* and *The Old Maid* with Bette Davis. I was a little disappointed. Where was the revolution that was convulsing the cinema?

That April sparkled. I sat on the café terraces with friends; I went for walks in the forest of Chantilly with Herbaud, who had

come back from London; our quarrel had evaporated of its own
accord. On the first of May it snowed, there were only a few stunted
slips of lily of the valley to buy on the street corners. But the air was
warm again that evening when the great V's stood out against the sky
and when all Paris was out in the streets singing and dancing.

Sartre was still in New York, Bost was in Germany. I spent the
evening with Olga, Mme Lemaire, Olga Barbezat, Vitold, Chauffard,
Mouloudji, Roger Blin, and a few others. We went to the Place de la
Concorde together on the métro; we were walking arm in arm, but as
soon as we came out onto the square, our little group was broken up;
I hung on to Mme Lemaire and Vitold, who kept groaning merrily:
"What an asshole game!" as the surging crowd carried us toward the
Place de l'Opéra; the opera house was streaming with red, white and
blue lights, flags were snapping and snatches of the *Marseillaise*
floated everywhere; we felt suffocated; one false step and we could
have been trampled where we stood. We made our way up toward
Montmartre and stopped at the Cabana Cubaine; what a crush! I can
still see Mme Lemaire walking over the tables to get to the ban-
quette where I managed to ensconce myself; Olga Barbezat, tears in
her eyes, was talking to me about my dear friends. Then we were out
in the street again, almost ready to give up. Where could we go?
Vitold and Mouloudji suggested the studio of one of their lady
friends. We set out; a jeep drew up to the sidewalk and offered us a
lift. Two G.I.s and two W.A.C.s went with us to visit Christiane
Lainier; the two W.A.C.s sat on a chest of drawers and nodded off,
while Mouloudji sang and Blin recited, very well, a poem by Milosz.
My recollection of this night is much more confused than my memories of our other, earlier festivities, perhaps because my feelings were
so confused. This victory had been won a long way off; we had not
awaited it, as we had the Liberation, in a fever of anxiety; it had
been foreseen for a long time, and offered no new hopes. It simply
marked the end of the war; in a way, this end was like a sort of death;
when a man dies, when time stops for him, his life hardens into a
single lump in which the years are superimposed and intermingled;
in much the same way, all the moments of the past were hardening
behind me: joy, tears, anger, grief, triumph, horror. The war was
over; it remained on our hands like a great, unwanted corpse, and
there was no place on earth to bury it.

And what was going to happen now? Malraux assured us that the
Third World War had just begun. All the anti-Communists were

anticipating disaster. Some optimists, on the other hand, foresaw eternal peace; thanks to technical progress, all nations would soon be united into one indivisible bloc. Personally I didn't think things were as rosy as that, but I didn't think we were going to start fighting again next week, either. One morning in the métro, I noticed some strange uniforms decorated with red stars: Russian soldiers. It was like seeing characters from a fairy tale. Lise, who spoke her native language fluently, tried to talk to them; they asked her sternly what she was doing in France, and her enthusiasm quickly waned.

A short while after VE Day, I spent a very happy evening with Camus, Chauffard, Loleh Bellon, Vitold, and a ravishing Portuguese girl named Viola. We left a bar in Montparnasse, which had just closed, and walked down to the Hôtel de la Louisiane; Loleh walked barefoot on the asphalt, saying: "It's my birthday, I'm twenty." We bought some bottles and drank them in the round room; the window was open to the warm air of the May night, and the people walking outside called out friendly words to us; for them, too, it was the first spring of peace. Paris was still as intimate as a village; I felt myself linked with all the unknown people who had shared my past, and who were as moved as I was by our deliverance.

Not everything was going so well, however. The material situation was not getting any better. Mendès-France had resigned. The charter of the C.N.R. had remained a dead letter. Camus, on his return from Algeria, described in *Combat* the exploitation of the natives, their poverty and their hunger; Europeans there were entitled to two-thirds of a pound of bread per day, Mohammedans to only a half pound, and even then they rarely got more than half of that. We heard very little about what had happened at Sétif: on May 8th, during the victory celebrations, *agents provocateurs*—Fascists, according to *Humanité*—had fired on the Mohammedans who had retaliated; the army had restored order; a hundred or so victims were rumored. It was not until much later that we learned the enormity of this lie.[1]

Ugly rumors were beginning to circulate about the prison camps liberated by the Americans. At first, bread and jam and sausages had been distributed with complete thoughtlessness. The inmates died like flies; now more care was taken, but the change of diet was still killing off large numbers. The fact was that none of the doctors knew

1 About eighty Europeans were massacred, after provocation on their part. The army raked the district: forty thousand dead.

how to treat the particular type of malnutrition found in the concentration camps, it was something entirely new; perhaps the Americans were less to blame than was thought at the time. There were also complaints about the dilatory way in which they were repatriating the internees. There was typhus at Dachau, people were dying there in hundreds; they were dying in all the camps; the French Red Cross had asked permission to enter them, but our allies had refused. This prohibition angered us. Furthermore, we found it intolerable that German prisoners should be well fed while the French population was dying of hunger. Our feelings toward our saviors had grown considerably colder since December.

Those who had been deported returned, and we discovered that we had known nothing. The walls of Paris were covered with photographs of charnel houses. Bost had gone into Dachau a few hours after the Americans; he could find no words to describe what he had seen. Another war correspondent told me for the first time about the death camps: "And the worst of it," he ended wildly, "is that they disgust you." Soon I saw pictures of them in the newspapers. There were a few short films made by the Americans, reports, eyewitness accounts, both written and oral: the death trains, the "selections," the gas chambers, the crematoria, the experiments of the Nazi doctors, the daily exterminations. When, fifteen years later, the Eichmann trial and its accompanying spate of films and books revived these already long-distant days, people were overwhelmed, they sobbed and fainted; in '45, we received these revelations in all their immediacy, they concerned our friends, our comrades, our own lives. What horrified me most was the bitter and futile struggle of the doomed to breathe for just one more second; the armored cars, the men pulling themselves up, already half-asphyxiated, toward the air outside, trampling on corpses, falling back dead; the ones who were slowly dying dragging themselves to work, collapsing, and being immediately finished off; the refusal to accept, the immense inanity of the refusal, and the last flicker so brutally stamped out; then nothing, not even the night.

Yvonne Picard did not come back; Alfred Péron died in Switzerland, a few days after being evacuated. Pierre Kaan was brought out of Buchenwald on May 10th. "At least I'll have seen the Germans defeated," he said; he died on May 20th. There was a rumor that Robert Desnos was on his way back; he died of typhus on June 8th, at Kerenice. Once more, I was ashamed to be alive. I was just as frightened of death as before; but those who do not die, I told myself with disgust, are accepting the unacceptable.

Sartre came back to Paris and told me about his trip. First, his arrival at the Waldorf; his lumber jacket and the clothes of the other journalists caused a sensation. A tailor had been summoned immediately. Then he told me about the cities, the country, the bars, the jazz; he had been shown around America by plane; in the Grand Canyon the pilot had asked every now and then: "Have I got room? Is the wing clear?" Sartre was a bit stunned by all he had seen. Apart from the economic system, segregation and racism, there were many things in the civilization of the Western Hemisphere that shocked him—the Americans' conformism, their scale of values, their myths, their optimism, their avoidance of anything tragic; but he had felt a great deal of sympathy for most of the people he had come into contact with; he had been greatly moved by the crowds of New York and felt that the people were worth more than the system. He had been very much struck by Roosevelt's personality during an interview the President had given to the French delegation a few days before his death. He was surprised to learn that certain intellectuals were worried about the rise of Fascism in the country; in various places, in fact, he had been told things that were by no means reassuring. During lunch one day, Ford's director of public relations had cheerfully referred to the coming war with the U.S.S.R. "But there's no frontier between America and Russia, where will you fight?" one of the Communist journalists asked. "In Europe," he replied, quite simply. This remark startled the French members, but they did not take it seriously. The American people did not appear to be at all bellicose. And so Sartre had abandoned himself to the pleasures of travel. He told me about the exiles he had met over there: in New York, Stépha and Fernand who was painting some very beautiful pictures; in Hollywood, Rirette Nizan who was earning a living writing subtitles for French films. He had met Breton, a remarkable man; he had met Léger too, whose style had changed considerably; Sartre liked his new paintings better than the old ones. A few days after his return, a huge black suitcase was dragged up to my room crammed full of clothes and food.

We continued to see lots of people. We enjoyed mixing with le Tout-Paris at previews and premieres, because the word Resistance, although it had lost its political power, still meant something among the intellectuals; when they found themselves side by side at these events, they were able to affirm their solidarity, and the performances had a value for us as demonstrations. In this atmosphere we saw *Murder in the Cathedral,* very well staged and acted by Vilar at the Vieux-Colombier, but boring. And *The Great Dictator,* which we had awaited so impatiently; almost everyone was disappointed; Hitler wasn't funny any more. René Leibowitz invited us to visit him one afternoon with the Leirises and played 12-tone music for us on his piano; I didn't understand it at all; but it had been forbidden by the Nazis and Leibowitz had lived in hiding for four years, every moment a miracle. It was at about the same time too, I think, that we went to the opening of the Gipsy in the Latin Quarter, where Mouloudji was making his début as a professional singer.

One evening I went with Sartre and the Leirises to the home of Dora Marr who painted very good pictures. She believed in table turning; we didn't; she suggested we give it a try. We all put our hands on a fairly large round table. Nothing happened, and it soon became rather tiresome. Suddenly the table began to shake, to move, to walk; we ran after it, our hands still joined and pressing down on top of it. The spirit informed us that it was Sartre's grandfather; the table spelled out the word *hell* with little knocks. For nearly an hour, running around the room or whirling around and around, it condemned us all to the everlasting fire and told things about Sartre that only he or I could possibly have known. Dora was exultant; the Leirises and Sartre were so stupefied they could only laugh. When we came out, I told them that it was I who had moved the table. Since I had been so sure it would not move, no one had suspected me.

In June, the Prix de la Pléiade was awarded for the second time. I was invited to take coffee with the members of the jury, who were all assembled at a luncheon at Gallimard's. I don't know who had forced on them the choice of author for the prize, but they all seemed upset. There were a great many people, bright sunlight, champagne, gin and plenty of whisky. Toward the end of the afternoon, sitting on the grass next to Queneau, I had a discussion with him about the "end of history." It was a frequent subject of conversation at the time. We had discovered the reality and weight of history, now we were wondering about its meaning. Queneau, who had been initiated into Hegelianism by Kojève, thought that one day all individuals would be reconciled in the triumphant unity of Spirit. "But what if I have a pain in my foot?" I said. *"We* shall have a pain in your foot," Queneau replied. We argued for a long time; and the alcohol fumes that were so pleasantly muddling our brains served only to make the dispute more vivacious; we decided to continue the following day and made a date. Queneau offered me a last drink; I knew my limit and declined; he insisted: "Just one glass of champagne." All right. He handed it to me, I drank it down and came to lying on a divan, my head burning and my stomach upset. Queneau had filled the glass I had drunk in one gulp with gin. I passed out immediately; it was very late, all the guests had gone home; only Sartre and the Gallimard family were still there; I was very ashamed and Jeanne tried to cheer me up as best she could. I was taken back to my hotel by car and went straight to bed. When I woke up twelve hours later, I was still in a bad way and had completely forgotten my date with Queneau; he hadn't remembered it either.

We drank hard in those days; first because the liquor was there, and also because it helped us find the relief we needed, it was part of the celebration; a strange celebration; close and appalling, the past was haunting us; looking ahead, we were torn between hope and doubt; no serenity was possible; the world opposed all our passions. We had to forget, and then even forget we were forgetting.

My sister and Lionel returned to Paris toward the end of May. During her years away she had done a great deal of work. She exhibited at Galerie Jeanne Castel—compositions inspired by things she had seen in Lisbon Hospital. I went with her to the Louvre, which was just reopening, and saw all the collections again. Sartre went out to the country with his mother, whose husband had died during the winter. I decided to go for a bicycling holiday; since Vitold was taking his holiday at the same time, we rode together for several days, side by side, from Paris to Vichy, along the gorges of the Creuse, then over the plateau of Millevaches and through the Auvergne. We talked about *Les Bouches Inutiles,* for which he had a theater in sight; we discussed possible rewriting and details of staging; Vitold was unhappy in his personal life, and told me about it. It was still difficult to find food and lodging; we had brought some canned American food with us which came in very handy for filling up after meals. We slept in back of a baker's shop, on café benches, and once we even slept in a charcoal burner's hut, practically in the open air. At Vichy I left Vitold and went up to the Vercors which I wanted to see for myself; it was then that I attended the great funeral feast at Vassieux that I described in *The Mandarins*.[1]

On August 7th—I had just got back to Paris—the A-bomb was dropped on Hiroshima. This meant the end of the war, and a revolting massacre; it heralded the possibility of perpetual peace, and also the possibility of the end of the world. We argued about it endlessly.

We spent a month at La Pouèze; we were there when the second bomb was dropped, when the Russians went into Manchuria and Japan capitulated. Sartre received letters that brought us echoes of the VJ Day celebrations in America. For us, the victory had been won in May.

For the first time I went abroad again with Sartre: to Bruges, to Antwerp, to Ghent. Things had always exceeded my imagination; now I realized that they also exceeded my memory. I began to taste the pleasure of reseeing. I had truly left one age of my life behind, and begun another.

1 There is one point in which that account is inexact. I described it as happening after the A-bomb, whereas in fact it took place a few days before.

CHAPTER II

BLOOD OF OTHERS WAS PUBLISHED in September; its main theme, as I have said, was the paradox of this existence experienced by me as my freedom and by those who came in contact with me as an object. This intention was not apparent to the public; the book was labeled a "Resistance novel."

Sometimes this misunderstanding irritated me, but I made the best of it, since the book's success far exceeded my expectations. It created much more of a stir than *She Came to Stay;* all the critics rated my second novel above my first; editorials expressing deep emotion were written about it in several newspapers. Both orally and by letter I received floods of compliments. Camus, though he liked the book, did not conceal his surprise at this success; as for Aron, he told me straight out, with the frankness of true friendship: "The fact is, I find this success revolting!" What he disliked, I think, was the approval I was receiving from the middle-of-the-road orthodox intellectuals who had made my book a sort of fad. Writers, journalists, intellectuals, still united by the events of the recent past, we were all inclined to indulge in mutual admiration; and apart from this, my novel was the first to speak quite openly about the Resistance. Nevertheless the reading public was not obeying orders from outside; the praise it showered on me was sincere; it read *Blood of Others* through the same spectacles that I had put on to write it.

Technically, I was under the impression that I had broken new ground; some congratulated me for it, others complained of the "long tunnel" which opens the book; everyone agreed that the form was original, for the French novel had up till then become largely a matter of respecting the rules. What I find even more surprising is that my narrative was said to be "bursting with blood and life." A book is a collective object. Readers contribute as much as the author to its creation; and mine, like myself, were concerned with morality; I had adopted a perspective so natural to them that they took what it showed them for reality itself. Beneath the veneer of abstract concepts and edifying sentences, they perceived the emotion so clumsily buried there; they brought it back to life; it was their own blood and their own life that they were lending to my characters. Then time passed; circumstances changed, and our hearts with them. Together we undid the work we had created together. Today there remains only a book whose defects can be seen at a glance.

It was labeled not only a "Resistance novel" but also an "Existentialist novel." Henceforth this label was to be affixed automatically to any work by Sartre or myself. During a discussion organized during the summer by the Cerf publishing house—in other words, by the Dominicans—Sartre had refused to allow Gabriel Marcel to apply this adjective to him: "My philosophy is a philosophy of existence; I don't even know what Existentialism is." I shared his irritation. I had written my novel before I had even encountered the term Existentialist; my inspiration came from my own experience, not from a system. But our protests were vain. In the end, we took the epithet that everyone used for us and used it for our own purposes.

So that, without having planned it, what we launched early that fall turned out to be an "Existentialist offensive." In the weeks following the publication of my novel, *The Age of Reason* and *The Reprieve* appeared, as well as the first numbers of *Les Temps Modernes*. Sartre gave a lecture—"Is Existentialism a Humanism?"—and I gave one at the Club Maintenant on the novel and metaphysics. *Les Bouches Inutiles* opened.[1] We were astonished by the furor we caused. Suddenly, in much the same way as one sees the picture in certain films breaking out of its frame and spreading to fill a wider screen, my life overflowed its old boundaries. I was pushed out into the limelight. My own baggage weighed very little, but Sartre was now hurled brutally into the arena of celebrity, and my name was associated with his. A week never passed without the newspapers discussing us. *Combat* printed favorable comments on everything that came from our mouths or our pens. *Terre des Hommes,* a weekly

[1] "In the same week, we have listened to a lecture by Sartre, attended the opening of *Les Bouches Inutiles* and read the first issue of *Les Temps Modernes*," wrote one surfeited critic in *Arts*.

started by Pierre Herbart and destined to survive only a few months, devoted numerous friendly or bittersweet columns to us in every number. Gossip about us and about our books appeared everywhere. In the streets, photographers fired away at us, and strangers rushed up to speak to us. At the Flore, people stared at us and whispered. When Sartre gave his lecture, so many people turned up that they couldn't all get into the lecture hall; there was a frenzied crush and some women fainted.

This uproar was partly a result of the "inflation" that Sartre was denouncing at that very moment[2]; now a second-class power, France was exalting her most characteristic national products with an eye on the export market: *haute couture* and literature. Even the humblest piece of writing was greeted by cries of acclaim, and its author immediately surrounded by an enormous fuss. Other countries were affected by the racket and seemed only too happy to make it even louder. However, if circumstances happened to be so favorable to Sartre it was no accident; there existed, at least at first glance, a remarkable agreement between what he was offering the public and what the public wanted. His petit-bourgeois readers had lost their faith too, in perpetual peace, in eternal progress, in unchanging essences; they had discovered History in its most terrible form. They needed an ideology which would include such revelations without forcing them to jettison their old excuses. Existentialism, struggling to reconcile history and morality, authorized them to accept their transitory condition without renouncing a certain absolute, to face horror and absurdity while still retaining their human dignity, to preserve their individuality. It seemed to offer the solution they had dreamed of.

In fact, it did not; and it was for this reason that Sartre's success was always as ambiguous as it was voluminous, bloated by its very ambiguity. People flung themselves avidly on nourishment that they were starved for; they broke their teeth on it and uttered howls that intrigued and attracted others by their violence. Sartre seduced them by maintaining, on the level of the individual, the rights of morality; but the morality he meant was not the same as theirs. His novels presented them with an image of society which they rejected; they accused him of sordid realism, of "miserabilism." They were prepared to listen to a few gentle truths about themselves, not to look themselves in the face. When confronted with Marxist dialectic, they

2 *La nationalisation de la Littérature*, in *Les Temps Modernes*, November 1945.

clamored for their freedom; but Sartre went too far. The freedom he offered them implied wearisome responsibilities; it could be turned against their institutions, against their mores; it destroyed their security. He invited them to use this freedom in order to ally themselves with the proletariat; they wanted to enter History, but not through that door. Labeled, pigeonholed, the Communist intellectuals worried them much less. In Sartre, the bourgeois recognized themselves without consenting to the self-transcendence he exemplified; he was speaking their language, and using it to tell them things they did not want to hear. They came to him, and came back to him, because he was asking the questions that they were asking themselves; they ran away because his answers shocked them.

A celebrity and a scandal at the same moment, it was not without uneasiness that Sartre accepted a fame which, exceeding all his old ambitions, also contradicted them. Although he had wanted posterity's approval, he had not expected to reach more than a very small public in his lifetime. A new fact, the advent of "one world," transformed him into an author of world fame; he had imagined that *Nausea* would not be translated for many years; as a result of modern techniques, the rapidity of communications, his works were already appearing in a dozen languages. It was a great shock for a writer reared in the old tradition, who had viewed the solitude of Baudelaire, of Stendhal, of Kafka, as the necessary price of their genius. Far from the circulation of his books being a guarantee of their worth, there were so many mediocre books achieving success that success seemed almost the sign of mediocrity. Compared to Baudelaire's obscurity, the inane glory that had burst upon Sartre had something annoying about it.

And its price was high. He received worldwide and unexpected attention, but saw himself robbed of that of future generations. Eternity had collapsed; the men of tomorrow had become the crabs Franz talks to in *The Condemned of Altona:* impervious, hermetic, radically alien. His books, even if they were read, would not be the ones he had written; his work would not remain. For him this was truly the death of God, who up till then had survived under the mask of words. Sartre owed this total catastrophe to his pride in accepting (assuming) it. He did so in his *Présentation* which opened the first number of *Les Temps Modernes* in October. Literature had shed its sacred character, so be it; henceforth he would posit the absolute in the ephemeral; imprisoned in his own epoch, he would choose that epoch against eternity, consenting to perish entirely along with it. This decision had more than one meaning. As a child, as an adolescent, Sartre's favorite fantasy had always been that of the *poète maudit,* misunderstood by all during his lifetime and struck by fame's lightning only beyond the grave, or perhaps, so he can enjoy it a little, on his deathbed; once more he was counting on the transformation of failure into triumph. His success had now overflowed all expectations, and in winning everything he had lost everything; by accepting that loss, he nourished the secret hope that everything would be restored. *"The rejection of posterity would give me posterity."*[1] Furthermore, at the age of forty, his highest ambitions had already, on one level, been satisfied; however ambiguous that success may have been, he would never exceed it. Repetition bored him; the best thing to do was to change his goals. Detesting passivity, if he preferred writing to actions, it was because he had never conceived of it as contemplation, as dream, as an escape from the self, but as construction. He had discovered, in the Stalag with *Bariona,* under the Occupation with *The Flies,* the vital role writing could play. When he renounced *being* and decided to *do,* to *make,* to *act,* he insisted that henceforth writing would always be a rallying cry, a commitment. This did not imply a contempt for literature but, on the contrary, the intention to restore its true dignity. If literature was in essence divine, then by toying with one's pen one could produce a sacred object; if it was human, then it could be kept from becoming degraded to the status of entertainment only by being identified with man's very existence, without dividing his life into various parts. Commitment (*engagement*), then, is simply the writer's total presence in what he has written.

This is a good example of the way in which Sartre could convince and outrage at the same time: his article provoked impassioned arguments that still continue today. In those troubled days when the world's rumors could violate even the most silent retreats, the public wanted nothing better than to fill the gap that separated journalism from literature, their daily interests from their cultural concerns; they were hungry for knowledge about this changed world they saw around them; they would satisfy this curiosity nobly if art seized upon these living, burning realities no academician had ever approached. But, they did not want to give up eternity. They wanted literature to transport them into those higher spheres where the

1 Unpublished notes.

work of art holds sovereign sway. Sartre respected literature to the point of identifying its destiny with that of humanity; to the public it seemed a sacrilege that he should bring it down from heaven to earth. It was the same in every realm. What he offered his readers enriched but disturbed them; and their resentment exceeded their gratitude.

He left himself wide open to attack by remaining faithful to the rule we had decided on: to react to the situation without assuming a role. He made no change in his habits; he lived in his hotel and in the cafés, he gave no thought to how he dressed, he avoided society; not only was he not married, but we both led such independent lives that it was impossible to think of our relationship as a classic example of "free love." All these eccentricities would have been forgiven if only Sartre had taken shelter behind his role as writer. He has never done so; and, in the surprise of his metamorphosis, it never occurred to him that he should at least take his new status into account. This simplicity earned him many friends. But public opinion was shocked. Ignorant of the real seriousness of a writer's work, the public only forgives him his privileges if he appears to them as the Other, flattering their taste for myths and idols and disarming envy. But the Other is the inhuman; the farces of vanity and prestige never suffice to hide the fact that the famous author is a man, a fellow being: he yawns, he eats, he walks—so many proofs that he is an impostor. A writer is hoisted up onto a pedestal only to scrutinize him more closely and conclude that it was a mistake to put him up there in the first place. All the same, as long as he hangs on up there, the distance between himself and the public will blunt the edge of their malice. Sartre wouldn't play the game, he stayed down with the crowd, with everyone, with anyone. Then, determined to identify him as the Other while noticing that he was just like them, people began to denounce him as a barefaced hoaxer. One evening, as we were coming out of the Golfe-Juan, one of the diners who had been eyeing Sartre malevolently all evening said to his wife: "Well, there you are! He blows his nose. . . ." All these grievances reinforced each other. Insofar as he was unable to conform to bourgeois behavior, his very simplicity became a weapon that could be used against him. The fact is that there was something suspect about it; it implied democratic convictions too extreme for the élite not to feel its superiorities were being challenged.

The idyl of the autumn of '44 was soon over. Nothing serious had been written about *Being and Nothingness*, but it was already being attacked in reviews, in classes, in lectures, by right-thinking people. On June 3, 1945, *La Croix* had denounced atheist Existentialism as "a graver danger than eighteenth-century Rationalism or nineteenth-century Positivism." The extreme Right was beginning, though still with some caution, to come out of hiding; in pamphlets, in newspapers, in gossip columns it started a rising flood of calumnies about Sartre. In November 1945, a blue-eyed young man in the Flore asked me to tell him about Sartre; he had to write an article about him in *Samedi-Soir*, a sensational weekly that had just been launched. I refused; he told me he would write the piece anyway, so he might as well get the information from me. I gave in and told him what he wanted to know. Several days later Sartre found a garbage can had been emptied over him: sordid and frivolous, his philosophy was fit for a sick people; morally and physically, his sole delight was filth. We were disconcerted by this display of mudslinging. But after all, what could you expect, such people would never be able to like us; we would learn to armor ourselves against their insults. When Boutang wondered in public if Sartre were a madman, we were unaffected. Sartre had torn himself away from his class, so the animosity it displayed toward him was natural. The animosity of the Communists, on the other hand, struck him as an injustice.

At their side, in June 1945, he had participated in the C.N.E. sale. ("Monsieur Sartre," one middle-aged lady had asked him, "according to you, Hell is other people?" "Yes . . ." "Well, myself, I'm Heaven," she said with a beatific smile.) He imagined that his *Mise au Point* had settled all their differences; he was mistaken. In an article that appeared in *Action*, Henri Lefebvre accused Sartre, in a very disagreeable tone, of demonstrating things in *Being and Nothingness* that for a Communist were self-evident; he was blocking the way to any philosophy of history and concealing from his readers all the really important problems. Kanapa contributed an article to the first number of *Les Temps Modernes*. "Come and see Maublanc with me," he said to Sartre. "Garaudy and Mougin want to talk to you about something." The morning of the interview, Kanapa telephoned in some embarrassment to say that he couldn't come. Sartre went to Maublanc's alone, where Garaudy and Mougin told him off: he was an idealist, he was turning young people away from Marxism; no Communists were writing for *Les Temps Modernes* any more. However, we had no wish to break with them. Politically, that fallacious entity, the Resistance, no longer existed. In December 1945, Malraux mentioned it in the Chamber of Deputies and caused noth-

ing but embarrassment, whereas a year earlier the mere word would
have produced an automatic burst of applause. The Resistance had
been split in three, and only the Communist Party sustained its revolutionary hopes; the rigid and anachronistic S.F.I.O. had been deserted by the masses. When the country, having voted for a Constituent Assembly with limited powers, proceeded to elections, the result
was a triumph for the Communists. Our aims were the same as
theirs, and they alone could achieve them. In the conflict between
Thorez and De Gaulle, we sided with the former.[1] We continued our
dialogue with the Communists. Merleau-Ponty expressed his views
in the November number of Les Temps Modernes; in December, Action replied harshly with an article entitled "Either-Or," and took
the same tone with Beaufret, who had written about Existentialism
in Confluences. Early in 1946, after Merleau-Ponty had published a
paper in Action on the nature of the hero in our time, he was informed in Cahiers d'Action that "the Communist is the permanent
hero of our time." Hervé attacked another article by Merleau-Ponty,
published in Les Temps Modernes, about political realism. Aliquié
and Naville debated, though in a more moderate tone, in the March
issue of the Revue Internationale. Since Existentialism's vogue
showed no signs of diminishing—the public came in droves to the
lecture Beaufret gave on it at the Vieux-Colombier in April—Action
finally decided to open a symposium: Must We Burn Kafka? directed
against littérature noire; fortunately the question roused many readers to indignation; among the replies there was only a single yes.
When we met Courtade, Hervé, Rolland or Claude Roy in private,
we always argued with good humor and seemingly on a basis of
mutual esteem; which made this public campaign all the more infuriating.

Of course Sartre was still far from having understood the fecun-
dity of the dialectical idea and of Marxist materialism; the works he
published that year are proof of that. His study of Baudelaire's écrits
intimes,[2] written two years earlier, is a phenomenological descrip-

---

[1] Thorez demanded one of the three major ministries for his party; De Gaulle
refused; a compromise was reached. But on January 22, 1946, De Gaulle resigned
because he disapproved of the Constitution drawn up by a Chamber of Deputies with
a Socialist and Communist majority.
[2] It was published in book form soon afterward with a preface by Leiris. Sartre's
intention—to understand the moments of a life through the totality of that life—es-
caped the critics (with the exception of Blanchot), who accused him of misunderstanding the nature of poetry.

tion; it lacks the psychoanalytical dimension that would have explained Baudelaire on the basis of his body and the facts of his life history. *Anti-Semite and Jew (Reflections on the Jewish Question)* shows how the phenomenological method can be enriched and made flexible by constant recourse to the social; but the concrete factual basis necessary to a history of anti-Semitism is not there. The article "Materialism and Revolution," which appeared in *Les Temps Modernes,* was a direct challenge to orthodox Marxism. Sartre criticized —with arguments less valid than those he would use today, but inspired by the same principles—the idea of a dialectic of nature; he analyzed materialism, in its strength and in its weaknesses, as a revolutionary myth. He indicated what status revolution necessarily and effectively grants the idea of freedom. At that point his line of thought stopped short, for he had not determined the freedom situation relation and was even more vacillating about history.

Less profound on certain points, on others more demanding than Marxist doctrine, Sartre's philosophy did not radically contradict it; he was seeking exchanges. The Communists rejected them. It is true that the bourgeois public interpreted Existentialism in such a way as to pervert its meaning; they regarded it—as they regarded the moralism of Camus—as a spare or emergency ideology. The Communists took the same view. Was this sectarianism forced on them by the political situation? The reasons are of little importance here. The fact is that intellectually a dialogue with Sartre was possible and that they chose instead to use for their own purposes the insults invented by the Right: poet of the sewers, philosopher of nothingness and despair. What hurt Sartre was that they thus transformed him into an enemy of the masses. *"Fame, for me, was hatred,"* he wrote later in his notes. It was a frustrating experience; with publicity far beyond his expectations, he had begun to exist for others; but as an object of hate, and as the hated. In 1945–46, he still hoped to change this situation; he no longer imagined that it would be easy.

I have often wondered what my position would have been if I had not been associated with Sartre in the way that I was. Close to the Communists certainly, because of my horror of all that they were fighting against; but I loved truth too much not to demand the freedom to seek it as I wished. I would never have become a Party member; since I had less objective importance than Sartre, the difficulties of this attitude would have been reduced, but the attitude itself would have resembled his. I therefore found myself in perfect agreement with him. Only, since it was not me the Communists were blaming, insulting, denouncing, since I was not personally compromised by their hostility, I was tempted to take it lightly. Sartre's tenacity in attempting to disarm it astonished me; sometimes I urged him to strike back. At other times, though, after a chance meeting or after reading something, I would wonder if we shouldn't have jettisoned our scruples as intellectuals and fought in the ranks of the Communist Party. Sartre too went through these periodic oscillations which sometimes coincided with mine and sometimes didn't. We argued a great deal.

I had never believed in the sacred nature of literature. God had died when I was fourteen; nothing had replaced him: the absolute existed only in the negative, like a horizon forever lost to view. I had wanted to become a legend, like Emily Brontë or George Eliot; but I was too firmly convinced that once my eyes had closed nothing would exist, to cling very tightly to such dreams. I would perish with the age I lived in, since I was going to die: there are not two ways of dying. I wanted to be widely read in my lifetime, to be esteemed, to be loved. Posterity I didn't give a damn for. Or I almost didn't.

I had grown used to living inside a writer's skin and nowadays scarcely ever caught myself looking at this new character and saying: It's me. But I enjoyed seeing my name in the papers, and for a while the fuss about us and my role as a "Parisian figure" gave me a good deal of amusement. In many ways, of course, I found it unpleasant. Not that I was oversensitive; when people called me "la grande Sartreuse" or "Notre-Dame de Sartre" I just laughed, but certain looks men gave me left their mark; looks that offered a lewd complicity with the Existentialist, and therefore dissolute, woman they took me for. To provide food for gossip, to titillate curiosity—that I did find repugnant. On the whole, however, I wasn't much affected by malice at the time and I enjoyed my newfound notoriety. It did not astonish me; it seemed to me quite normal that the Liberation should have transformed my life along with the rest of the world. Nor did I exaggerate it: it was very slender compared with Sartre's. I observed this difference without envy, because he meant too much to me for me to be jealous of him, and also because it seemed to me quite justified. I didn't even regret not having deserved more; my first book had only come out two years before, it was not yet time to start adding up scores. The future lay before me, and I had faith in it. Where would it take me? I avoided questioning myself about the value of my work, in the future as in the present. I wanted neither to surround myself with illusions, nor to run the risk of a possibly cruel lucidity.

All things considered, unlike Sartre, I jeopardized myself neither as writer nor in my social reality. I could pride myself on having been less deceived than he by the illusion of being, for I had paid the price of this renunciation during my adolescence; and I could reproach myself with having refused to confront my objective existence; there is no doubt that my skepticism helped me evade the difficulties that Sartre was coming to grips with. This escape was made easier for me by my temperament. I had always taken more pleasure in the immediate than he. I enjoyed all the pleasures of the body, the feel of the weather, walks, friendships, gossip, learning, seeing. And also, far from being saturated by success as he was, I could see no limits to my hopes; I was satisfied but not satiated. Circumstances assured every effort and even the slightest success a resonance that stimulated me further; tasks presented themselves, and also the means of performing them. The present and its near horizons were enough for me.

For some time our review took all my attention. Thanks to Sartre's renown and to the controversy his theory of *engagement* provoked, we had a great many readers; our aim was to reflect an epoch which sought to know itself, and *Les Temps Modernes* had a lasting success. Paulhan, who had edited the N.R.F. for many years, gave us the benefit of his experience; he usually made up most of the numbers, and he taught me the technique. Aron, who had acquired a lot of experience with *La France Libre,* also gave us technical advice; he followed the progress of *Les Temps Modernes* very closely, trusting, I think, that Sartre would not have the perseverance to find it interesting for long and that he would then take over. He was chiefly concerned with the political section and was very skillful at finding reasons for not publishing articles favorable to Communism. Excellent as an analyst, he was pathetic as a prophet: he announced a Socialist triumph on the eve of an election that was a landslide for the M.R.P. and a defeat for the S.F.I.O. Leiris was in charge of poetry, and our tastes rarely coincided. The committee met often and argued hotly.

I have said what the review meant to Sartre. Everything in this world is a sign that points back to everything: our originality lay in our search for facts that were both banal and revealing. Further, we hoped to influence our contemporaries by our choice of texts and by the orientation of our articles. Besides which, it was very useful to have at hand the means of expressing immediately our impatience, our surprise, our approval. A book takes a long time to write and, in those days, a long time to publish; in a review, it is possible to catch the news on the wing, to address one's friends and refute one's adversaries almost as quickly as in private correspondence. I would read an article that made me angry and say to myself immediately: "I must answer that!" That's how all the essays I wrote for *Les Temps Modernes* came into being. In this groping, seething period of renascence, there were always new problems presenting themselves, challenges to be taken up, errors to be rectified, misunderstandings to be cleared up, criticisms to be answered. Very few books and reviews were being published; our polemics had the intimacy, the urgency and the warmth of family quarrels.

I wanted very much to see *Les Bouches Inutiles* put on. At the preview of *No Exit,* I had been stirred by the thunder of the applause; it was much more immediate, more intoxicating than the scattered echoes wakened by a book. I had been to see Camus' *Caligula* which had left me cold when I read it. Gérard Philipe transformed the play. I wanted my own play to undergo a similarly flattering metamorphosis. And then I yielded once more to illusions: my name on the métro cards would be the name of a playwright, and the playwright would be me. When Vitold suggested a meeting with Serge who ran the Théâtre du Carrefour, I accepted greedily.

Ten years earlier, at Rouen, I had heard about a handsome young man whom everyone had been in love with; he had married the prettiest of my third-year students; his name was Serge: this was the man. Olga knew him; when she saw him again, she exclaimed: "Serge! It's you!" "Well, yes," he said apologetically. He was older, fatter and had lost a lot of hair. He had been divorced and had married again, this time Jacqueline Morane, who wanted to play the part of Catherine. She had stage presence and a lovely voice. Serge decided to produce my play; no sooner had rehearsals begun than he told me he was going to have to stop. He was short of money; could I put my hands on any? It wasn't easy. Because of the paper shortage, books were printed only in editions of five thousand; our normal income was enough to allow us to live comfortably, but with nothing left over. I was just thinking that all was lost when, quite unexpectedly, a fortune fell out of the sky.

Nero[1] had been released from Fresnes early that year, and I had seen him three or four times since then, at the Brasserie Lipp, at the Flore, at the Deux Magots. He would have liked to work in some capacity for *Les Temps Modernes*, but there was nothing we could give him to do. "In that case, my only salvation is to write," he said to me; the tameness of the samples he showed me left little hope in that direction. Yet when he told me about one of his latest suicide attempts, he spoke with great artistry: a hundred aspirin tablets swallowed one by one, the slowness, the lugubriousness of this operation, which ended with his throwing up. He had made other attempts with barbiturates. Each time he managed to leave himself an emergency exit, while taking considerable risks all the same. "It's not a game, it's not an act," he explained. "There's a state of indifference you reach with regard to both life and death: you have to give death its chances."

One October morning, he pushed open the door of the Flore. "I know you need money," he said. He must have heard this from Renée, whom I saw from time to time. He put down a bundle of notes on the table in front of me—a hundred thousand francs; it was a lot in those days. "Don't worry, it's mine. I earned it." Renée had told me Nero had found a good job, and he was so persuasive with people that I was scarcely even surprised; he was connected with the ministry responsible for reconstructing disaster areas and was in charge of estimates. By financing *Les Bouches Inutiles,* he hoped he would be making up to some extent for the nasty trick he had played on Sartre. I took the money straight to Serge.

At seven the following morning, there was a knock on my door: "Police!" Two cops came into my room and ordered me to go with them to the Quai des Orfèvres; I was accused of receiving stolen goods, and I would have to return the hundred thousand francs. I dressed and ran along the corridor to let Sartre know; he could go and borrow the money from Gallimard. We were intrigued. What new scheme had Nero thought up? And why had he mixed me up in it? In any case I was to blame. The government wasn't going to put a notorious con man in charge of their estimates; my desire to see my play performed had clouded my judgment.

At the Quai des Orfèvres I was seated in a vast room furnished with tables and benches. I had brought some work with me, and for

[1] Cf. *The Prime of Life.*

three or four hours I wrote. Inspectors came in and out, bringing people accused of various offenses and questioning them; baskets of sandwiches were passed around; between interrogations, they ate and chatted. Toward noon, one of them told me to follow him; he took me to the office of a magistrate to whom Sartre had just given the money and who asked us for our autographs. The next day, all the newspapers printed the story. One journalist introduced his piece with the ingenious headline: "Cruel as his homonym, Nero hands the Existentialists over to the cops."

Nero gave his explanation. He obtained—he didn't say how—the names of people who had suffered war damages and who were suspected of having made false declarations. Furnished with false papers, he would threaten them with heavy fines and imprisonment, then he would let it be understood that his silence could be bought. To others who had not yet put in their claims, he would suggest that they pad them a bit: a small bribe and he would approve them. Here too, his victims' complicity would assure his impunity, or so he thought; but nevertheless his machinations were brought to light. He had not committed forgery and could only be accused of fraud because he had avoided imitating official papers exactly and had changed the placing of the red, white and blue band running across them. Caught unexpectedly, and under pressure to return the money, he had thought it would seem more honorable to have invested his profits in an artistic venture than to have squandered them, and so he brought me into it; at least, that's how he explained it to me. He was only in prison a short time; I saw him again afterward, but not often. All the deals he managed to pull off after that were pretty small-time. Now and then he would try to kill himself. One day, he made up his mind to do it properly. He was found in his hotel room, lying on his bed with Renée's photo on his chest, finished off by a massive dose of prussic acid.

Les Bouches Inutiles was put on after all. I attended rehearsals; I was so amazed to hear my lines become real voices that it all seemed perfect. Only one thing disappointed me. I had expected it to be staged so that one scene would follow another in a flash; but each one had a separate set. The theater was poor and didn't have many stagehands; when Sartre saw a run-through, the slowness of the scene changes worried him, but I was assured that they would be fast enough when the time came. However, on the afternoon of the dress rehearsal, the performance was delayed by infuriating waits, and I grew more uneasy. I had amused myself by playing a harmless enough game; suddenly, there were witnesses, judges, turning it into a public event for which I was responsible; I had invited them, words sprung from my pen were assailing their ears. I was ashamed of my immodesty; at the same time, their view superimposed itself on my own; I could no longer see clearly. At certain lines, too naïvely inspired by Existentialist philosophy, friends winked at each other. I was sitting next to Genet, who is never tactful with his criticisms. "This isn't what the theater's about! This isn't theater at all," he whispered in my ear. It was agony. However, after the final curtain, I was congratulated and my confidence returned. On opening night, watching through a hole in the curtain as the audience came in, I was anxious but optimistic. Once more my friends were encouraging and it seemed to me that the applause was quite enthusiastic. A play is not inert like a book; something had happened, through me, to a great number of people—director, actors, stagehands; something good, I thought. I had planned a supper in Gégé's apartment, my guests were all very gay and, with the help of the whisky, I felt quite elated. Jacques Lemarchand took me aside; he deplored all those static scenes, those dead waits; and then, with one or two exceptions, he had found the actors inadequate; the play's qualities didn't come across, whereas its defects came across only too well. Knowing his kindliness, I lost my confidence. What were the less well disposed critics going to say?

The dailies tore me to pieces almost unanimously; it was a pretty harsh disappointment. The weeklies were less hostile; I even found some warm defenders: Philippe Hériat, who devoted two articles to me; the critic of *Lettres Françaises,* who talked about Cornelian theater; and the critic of *Terre des Hommes. Action* condemned the play's morality but was more or less favorable. Word of mouth was not too bad; the audiences kept coming for several weeks. Then it got cold and the theater was very badly heated; it was also poorly situated: every now and again the noise of the elevated métro trains drowned out the actors. Receipts began to drop; after fifty performances, the theater closed. This setback didn't hit me too hard. Without blinding myself to the play's defects, I did think it hadn't really had a fair chance. There were people who liked it; naturally I was more inclined to give their opinions more weight than those of the people who didn't. Above all, there were too many interests beckoning me on to linger over my regrets.

Bost came back from America, where he had been sent as a reporter by *Combat;* he was exultant. Lise had got engaged to a G.I. whom she was getting ready to join in the States; she was eager to get out of France, where there was no future for her and where she was hungry. Sartre was also going back to New York. In January, he had met a young woman there, half-separated from her husband and, despite her brilliant position in the world, not very satisfied with her life; they had been very attracted to each other. When told about my existence she had decided that when he went back to France they should forget each other; his feelings for her were too strong for him to accept this; he had written to her from Paris and she had replied. In order to see her again, he had had himself invited back by some American universities; on December 12th, he embarked on a Liberty ship.

I should have liked to leave Paris. The food situation was still bad; in the little restaurants I frequented, I never had enough to eat. I couldn't find anywhere to work; in my room, I was cold; at the Flore, too many people knew me; since we had begun *Les Temps Modernes*, which had its offices at Gallimard's, we had been going a lot to the bar of the Pont-Royal, which was nearby; it was warm and quiet in that gilded basement room, but it was inconvenient trying to write on the casks they used for tables. I had a carbuncle on my leg which incapacitated me for several days. The Alliance Française had invited me to give some lectures in Tunis and Algiers, but this time the Relations Culturelles didn't give me any help in getting there: there was never room for me on either the boats or the planes, which were very infrequent anyway, leaving for Tunis.

I went to the preview of *The Brothers Karamazov*: Vitold was playing Ivan, Dufilho, Smerdiakov, and Maria Casarès was a delicious Grushenka. I saw Camus quite often. One evening, after we had both eaten at the Brasserie Lipp and drunk at the bar of the Pont-Royal until closing time, he bought a bottle of champagne and we emptied it together at the Louisiane, talking till three in the morning. Because I was a woman—and therefore, for he was quite feudal about such things, not quite an equal—he would end up telling me intimate secrets about himself; he gave me bits of his notebooks to read and told me about the difficulties in his private life.

There was one theme that preoccupied him, and he often came back to it: someday he must write the truth! The fact is that in his case there was a much greater gap than for many others between his life and his work. When we went out together, drinking, laughing, chatting, late into the night, he was funny, cynical, rather coarse and often very bawdy in his conversation; he would admit his emotions, give way to his impulses; he was capable of sitting down in the snow on the edge of the sidewalk at two in the morning and meditating pathetically about love. "You have to choose. Love either lasts or it goes up in flames; the tragedy is that it can't last and go up in flames as well." I liked the "hungry ardor" with which he abandoned himself to life and pleasure, I liked his enormous consideration for others: when Bost was a war correspondent, every time Camus received a dispatch from him he immediately telephoned Olga. And yet, on the staff of *Combat,* he was accused of being arrogant and peremptory. During serious discussions, he would close up and become very formal, replying to arguments with noble phrases, high-flown sentiments, righteous rages it seemed to give him great satisfaction to produce. Pen in hand, he became a rigid moralist who seemed to have nothing in common with our happy nocturnal companion. He was aware that his public image utterly failed to coincide with the truth of his private self, and this occasionally embarrassed him.

Tired of dragging about Paris, I went skiing in Mégève; I returned to the Chalet Idéal-Sport and was moved to open my eyes in the morning and recapture the white splendor of the high snows, the memories of another age. For those times, today long gone and flattened by the weight of time, like contours of the earth seen from a high-flying plane, still had varying depths then, to the eye of memory; the past, still fresh but already strange, was amazing. "Six years ago," I wrote to Sartre, "I wrote you from here and the war was on. It seems much longer ago than six years. I feel in some way out of things, as though in another life; I don't recognize either myself or the world as it was then any more. And yet there are still memories, the memories I shared with you in that first life. But they have so little connection with the present that they have a strange, rather painful effect."

I had company; Lefèvre-Pontalis, one of Sartre's ex-pupils who had been a friend of Bourla's, had brought his wife to a little hotel on the slope of Mont d'Arbois; shortly after my arrival, Bost arrived at the Idéal-Sport with Olga and Wanda; the two women only ven-

tured onto the ski slopes now and then, they preferred sunbathing.
Salacrou was staying right over my head, Chez Ma Tante. He was a
much better skier than all of us, but often came for a drink. Sometimes, in the morning before the ski lifts had started working, I
would go down the deserted slopes to Saint-Gervais, alone in the silence and the cold. But generally I only went out during the afternoon; before lunch I worked at *All Men Are Mortal*, surrounded by
the vast, glittering landscape of the mountains. Up till then I had
always been too strict ever to mix work and play; now I found the
combination very pleasant. After the continual agitation of Paris,
the calm of the chalet suited me. "I feel so relaxed with no one looking at me and no one talking to me!" I wrote Sartre. All the same, I
was very flattered when the lady who owned the chalet said to Bost:
"But she's very well known, Mlle de Beauvoir; any number of people ask if that's who she is; it's the same as with M. Salacrou."

Finally I got a message that I had been allotted a seat on a plane
leaving from Marignane three days later; I hurried back to Paris,
which seemed very dreary. "Paris is icy, the hotel isn't heated, and
there seems to be absolutely nothing to eat. It doesn't get light before
nine in the morning and there's no electricity; all the bars close at
ten; everyone looks mournful, and the whole thing is intolerably
boring and miserable," I wrote Sartre. I leapt joyfully into the train
that was to take me to Pas-des-Lanciers, where a bus picked me up
and took me to the airport; it was early in the morning. I was slightly
nervous. I had never been a in a plane before but how marvelous, I
thought, not only that there should still be first times left for me, but
that they should be happening!

Alas! Someone had taken my seat, and the next plane didn't leave
for three days. I hadn't a cent on me, it was drizzling, they were
counting on me in Tunis, and my anger only served to increase my
despair. I pleaded, the pilots relented and made a place for me between them in the cockpit; it was a maiden flight far beyond my
wildest dreams. To the left, to the right, in front of me, out to
infinity shone the Mediterranean Sea, and it seemed to me miraculous to look down on it from so high in the sky. *We used to say to
each other: some day, when we're rich, we'll take the plane to London; but they say you're ill most of the way, and in any case you can
scarcely see a thing.* I soared over the mountains of Corsica without
having had to climb them; I could make out people, sheep. Then the
outline of Sardinia appeared against the sea's blue, as precise as it was

in my childhood atlas. Suddenly there were stucco houses below, flat roofs, palm trees, camels: Africa and my first plane landing.

There was no one waiting for me at the airport; so much the better; this unexpected freedom, this incognito arrival enchanted me; coming from the gray atmosphere of Paris, the *souks* were as fresh-looking as the ones in Tetuán, once upon a time.

The next day, the representative of the Alliance Française, M.E., took me in hand; his wife looked like Kay Francis. They found me a room at the Tunisia-Palace; they took me by car to Carthage, to Hammamet. At Sidi-bou-Saïd we had to walk ten yards to reach the sea and a magnificent panorama; they had brought Julien Benda here and he had refused to leave the car. "I can imagine, I can imagine . . ." he had said. I hoped I would never become indifferent to such things.

I certainly wasn't then. The whole time not devoted to my lectures and to the unavoidable social functions, I spent on expeditions. I went, alone, to visit the Roman ruins at Dougga. My hosts were worried; a year earlier, a teacher had been raped and butchered on this road. For my outing the following day, they suggested I go to Gramat, quite near Tunis; there was a little hotel, at the sea's edge, and sun-covered dunes where, after lunch, I lay down with a book. I dropped off to sleep and, half-dreaming, I thought: "How odd! There are cats on these dunes." I opened my eyes: no cats, but a very dirty old Arab sitting on my stomach; in the sand next to his basket, a knife. "Better raped than butchered," I said to myself, but I was almost fainting with terror. As I pushed him off I suggested, extremely volubly, that he might like some money; he hesitated. I emptied my purse into his hands and ran, slipping and stumbling, out of the dunes as fast as my legs would carry me; fortunately I had left the greater part of my fortune at the Tunisia-Palace. I told the woman at the hotel that I had met an old tramp; she knew him—a petty thief who used his knife for cutting asparagus. I supposed afterward that he had attacked me without much conviction, simply because he felt he oughtn't to miss an opportunity.

My stay in Tunis was pleasant; the E.'s took me to the nicest restaurants. One evening we went to dinner at the house of Bernard Zherfuss, the architect, the brother of one of my friends with whom I had studied at Désir; he was married. I had made some progress in psychology; in spite of their utter discretion, it seemed to me that something intangible passed between him and Mme E. I was to learn, a year or two later, that they had each sought a divorce and then married each other.

The E.'s regarded French policy in Tunisia as clumsy; they were in favor of a *rapprochement* between the French and Moslem middle classes. At their house I met Tunisian women dressed, made up, groomed and scented just like Parisiennes; they no longer wore veils except in the morning, to go to market; they were eager for their liberty. Among the men, the young ones were on their side; they resented having their fathers choose wives for them who were ignorant and unenlightened. No one had anything to tell me about the Franco-Tunisian situation in general, and I did not question them too closely. The demon of adventure had possessed me again. I was getting ready to explore Tunisia and then go back up to Algiers through the Sahara; the transportation situation was so unreliable that it was a risky undertaking, but that only whetted my appetite.

Sousse, Sfax, the great Roman Circus of El Djem, Kairouan, Djerba—I reached them all without difficulty by train, by bus and by boat. At Djerba, Ulysses had forgotten Penelope and Ithaca: the island was worthy of its legend. It was a cool orchard with a carpet of dappled grass; the glossy crowns of the palms sheltered the delicate blossoming trees; the edges of this garden were lashed by the sea. I was the only guest in the hotel, and the owner spoiled me. She told me that the summer before, one of her boarders, a little English girl, had gone every day to a deserted beach to lie in the sun; one day she came back to lunch, her face all crumpled, and did not touch her food. "What's the matter?" my hostess asked; the girl burst into tears. Three Arabs, who had been watching her for several days, had raped her, one by one. "I tried to cheer her up," the woman said. "I said to her: Oh! Mademoiselle, when you're traveling . . . Come now, calm yourself; after all, when you're traveling!" But she had insisted on packing her bags the same evening. Obviously rape is no myth around here, I thought; there are many men who live in such extreme poverty that marriage, and therefore a woman, are denied them. Their loins cry out; and then, they're used to the veils, the modesty of Moslem women; a woman stretched out on the sand, half nude, is offering herself, she is a woman there to be taken. After that, to go into the village, where there was a fair the following day, I accepted the services of an escort, a bearded old man whose virtue my hostess had guaranteed.

To continue my journey I had to avail myself of military transport; I stopped at Médenine, where I saw those curious vaulted granaries, stuck one on top of the other, called "gorfa"; the captain promised me that the day after next a truck would take me on to Matmata; then I took another bus on to Tatahouine: this alarming name attracted me. As I got down from the bus, a spahi in ceremonial dress very formally prevailed on me to follow him. He accompanied me as far as a villa, furnished with cushions and carpets, which was the home of the A.I. commander, a bearded Breton with very blue eyes; someone in Médenine had forewarned him of my arrival and he let it be understood that there was no question of my going around alone and on foot while I was in his territory; such behavior would cast a slur on the good name of France. If I went out it would be under escort and in a jeep. I yielded to his decision. I was seated at a table where he was dining with the other officers of the A.I. and a lady doctor whose husband, also a doctor, was away; I was flabbergasted by the outrageousness of her language and her jokes, which the male members of the party lapped up with scandalized laughter—what a virago! I was given a bedroom adjoining hers; she became quite different. She explained to me that her extreme freedom of speech was a protection against advances and coarseness. She worked very hard; her main task was the treatment of the venereal diseases which infested the population; she had artificially inseminated the wives of the caïd, who was incapable of getting them with child himself. A strange life, which she led at a great pace, though not without finding it wearisome. She told me that the officers of the A.I. never mixed with the officers of the Legion; they formed a small, closed circle of their own. They rode; they went to Gabès from time to time. They were unutterably bored.

No doubt that explained the warmth with which I was received: any diversion was a welcome one. In the morning they took me across landscapes whose glaring nakedness already presaged the desert; at noon they organized a great *méchoui;* we went to look at troglodyte villages hollowed out of cliffs the color of dawn; the notables invited us into their caves hung with rich rugs, offered us hard-boiled eggs which it would have been offensive to refuse, but which I simply couldn't get down; I made a cache of them in my purse. In the evening, it appeared that the captain had made inquiries about me and I was asked to talk about Existentialism; they had invited the local teacher. I can't remember what I stammered out.

At Médenine, the promised truck was waiting for me. I was the

only passenger. The driver must have known the Matmata road before it was damaged in the war. In two or three places bridges had
been blown up, but he managed to ford the wadis and eventually got
me to that strange village where ten thousand people live under the
ground. The marketplace was a seething mass; nothing but men,
swathed in snowy burnouses, chattering and happy; the dark, blue-
eyed women, some young and beautiful, but all sad-looking, were to
be found at the bottom of the many shafts which opened onto the
caves; I visited one of these dungeons. Down in these dark, smoky
caverns I saw crowds of half-naked children, a toothless old woman,
two dirty-looking middle-aged women, and a pretty girl covered with
jewelry who was weaving a carpet. As I came back up into the light, I
passed the master of the house returning from market, resplendently
healthy and dazzling in his white burnous. I pitied my sex.

I slept at Gabès; the man who owned the hotel slipped a poem
under my door in which he deplored, between courtly compliments,
the fact that I was an Existentialist. I was disappointed by the oasis at
first; I found myself walking along muddy roads between earth walls,
and except for the palms overhead, I couldn't see a thing. Then I
managed to slip into the orchards and discovered the gaiety of fountains amid flowering trees. The gardens of Nefta were even more
delicate. On one side of the main square, there was a charming hotel.
In the visitors' book, Gide had written: "Had I known Nefta, I
should have loved it more than Biskra."[1] Next morning, I sat on the
sunny terrace reading Koestler's *Spartacus* while I waited for the
truck that was to take me into the heart of the desert. The driver, a
Tunisian, made me sit beside him: there was no other woman among
his passengers, and no European. Before long, I was surprised to see
the road fading out; we were going straight over the dunes. It had
been explained to me that in order to drive on sand you have to let
some air out of the tires, and then have the requisite knack; begin-
ners always break down after the first hundred yards. Our driver
seemed to be an expert; all the same, every time he hurled the truck
toward a dune, I thought: He'll never get to the top. At the top, the
truck would pause for an instant at a very precarious angle. It's going
to turn over, I thought. Then it would continue down; and we'd
begin all over again. The dunes spread in waves as far as the eye
could reach in all directions, and I asked myself: "Why is it so beautiful?" The sand stretching to infinity gave the impression of a

---

[1] I quote from memory.

smooth, simple world, formed from surface to center out of a single substance; a delightful play of curves and light breathed, like music, from the serenity of the One.

I walked in the moonlight at El Oued; the earth was hollowed out into vast funnels with gardens buried at the bottom; from a distance, there was something charmingly fantastic about seeing the crowns of the palm trees sprouting straight out of the sand. I spent the day on the crest of a dune; the women from a nearby *douar* climbed up and encircled me; they opened my purse, played with my lipstick, undid my turban, while the children played tag with great shrieks across the sand. I never tired of contemplating the calm monotony of those tall, motionless waves. On a bench in the public square, I was shown the name of Gide, carved with his own hand.

I was delayed at Ouargla for three days. I wanted to go on to Ghardaïa. A date merchant was waiting for a truck that was supposed to take a shipment for him; every morning I crossed the fantastic esplanades thought up by a homosexual colonel—Colonel Carbillet—who had evidently thought he was Lyautey. I would ask the merchant: "Has the truck arrived?" "No. But it's sure to be here tomorrow. . . ." I would go back to the hotel, where I was the only guest, and they would feed me camel; I liked sitting on the terrace, moored at the edge of the undulating sands. I had nothing left to read, and all I could find in the village was an old number of *La Bataille;* there were moments when it seemed that time had ceased to exist, and I felt a strange weakness come over me; at those moments I would go out, my sandals in my hand, into the swell of the apricot-colored dunes, intercepted far away by hard, pink cliffs. Under the palms a veiled woman would pass silently, or an old man with a donkey; it is beautiful to see a human being pass across the motionless face of nature without disturbing it; I would come back toward my hotel and be moved to see my own footprints in the soft sand. After years of living with others, this encounter with myself stirred me so deeply that I believed it to be the dawn of a sort of wisdom. It was only an interim, but for a long time I kept the palm trees, the sands, and their silence in my heart.

They were expecting me in Algiers; I decided to forego Ghardaïa. In the bar of the Grand Hôtel at Touggourt I uneasily rediscovered a civilization I had forgotten: restless, verbose, gluttonous. I left the next day, not by the express that most Europeans take, but—because I wanted to stop off at Biskra for a few hours—by a much earlier, slower train almost exclusively filled with Arabs. All the cars were packed; a cluster of people hung from every footboard; I managed to get up onto a platform where I stood, lashed by gusts of sand. I hadn't had time to get a ticket; I asked the conductor for one. "A ticket? Do you really want one?" He laughed and shook his head. "You're a European! You don't have to pay." I marveled at this logic: since I had money, he wasn't going to ask me for it. But the natives he treated abominably; the ones who were hanging on to the buffers he knocked off and sent sprawling onto the ground; the train didn't go very fast and they weren't hurt, but they stared despairingly at the desert surrounding them, yelled and shook their fists.

Biskra was less attractive than it is in Gide's books. Constantine, rainy and full of hate, chilled my spirits. In Algiers I was never left on my own and saw nothing but "sights." To my eyes, still dazzled by the Sahara, the north seemed dull.

I came back by plane and found Paris deserted. Sartre hadn't returned, Lise had gone, Olga was staying in Normandy with her parents, Bost was traveling in Italy with a group of journalists, Camus was about to go to New York. I worked, I moped a bit. Through Queneau I met Boris Vian. Trained as an engineer, he wrote and played the trumpet; he had been one of the guiding spirits of the zazou movement engendered by the war and the Collaboration: since their rich parents spent most of the year in Vichy, these young upper-middle-class boys and girls organized anarchistic parties in the abandoned family apartments; they emptied the wine cellars and broke the furniture, imitating the plundering soldiers; they bought and sold on the black market. Anarchistic, apolitical, they reacted against their Pétainist families by flaunting an aggressive anglophilia; they imitated the stiff elegance, the accent, the manners of English snobs. America counted so little for them that they were abashed when Paris was suddenly filled with Americans; however, they had one very strong bond with them: jazz, about which they were fanatical. The Abadie band, in which Vian played, was hired by the "French Welcome Committee" on the very first day the Americans entered Paris, and was then attached to the Special Service Show. This explains the way the ex-zazous dressed for the next three years: American surplus blue jeans and checked shirts. They used to meet on the Avenue Rapp, near the Champs-Élysées, and also at the Champo at the corner of the Rue Champollion, which was a dance hall at the time. A handful of them not only liked jazz but also

Kafka, Sartre and American novels; during the war they rummaged through the bookstalls along the Seine and were triumphant if they dug out some forbidden work by Hemingway or Faulkner. To read and talk, they came to Saint-Germain-des-Prés. That's how I met Vian at the bar of the Pont-Royal; a manuscript of his was being read by Gallimard, and Queneau thought highly of it; I had a drink with them and with Astruc; it seemed to me that Vian listened to himself too much and that he was too inclined to cultivate paradoxes for their own sake. He gave a party in March; by the time I arrived, everyone had already had quite a bit to drink; his wife, Michelle, her long, silky blond hair spread over her shoulders, was smiling beatifically; Astruc was asleep barefoot on the divan; I too drank manfully while we listened to American records. At about two in the morning, Boris offered me a cup of coffee; we sat down in the kitchen and talked on into the dawn: about his novel, about jazz, about literature, about engineering, which was his trade. I no longer found anything affected in that long, pale, smooth face, but instead great kindliness and a sort of stubborn candor; Vian was as vehement about hating what he called *"les affreux"* as he was about liking what he liked. He played the trumpet in spite of the fact that it was bad for his heart. ("If you go on, you'll be dead in ten years," his doctor had told him.) We talked on and the dawn came too quickly: I valued beyond price these fleeting moments of eternal friendship.

A month later, the first Gallimard cocktail party was given; Astruc went to sleep behind a sofa; when he woke up the room was empty; he tried to feel his way out, stumbled into the dining room, where the Gallimard family had just gathered for dinner, and stuck both his hands in the soup tureen.

One of the people I saw often was Merleau-Ponty, with whom I was working on *Les Temps Modernes.* I had reviewed his thesis on *The Phenomenology of Perception* for the magazine. Our middle-class religious backgrounds created a bond between us, but we reacted to them in different ways. He still retained a nostalgia for a lost paradise; I did not. He liked being with older people and mistrusted the young, whereas I greatly preferred them to their elders. His writing revealed a sense of nuance, and he talked hesitantly; I was for clear-cut opinions. He was interested in the peripheries of thought, in the nebulous fringes of existence rather than in its hard core; with me it was the opposite. I had great respect for his books and essays, but it seemed to me that he didn't understand Sartre's thinking very

well. I brought to our discussions a vehemence to which he submitted with a smile.

Toward the middle of March, Olga came back from Normandy;
the family doctor, unable to account for her fever and lassitude, had
had her X-rayed: both her lungs were infected. The failure of *Les
Bouches Inutiles* had been a violent setback for her, and her sunbathing at Mégève had not been beneficial. I cabled Bost, who came
home immediately. The specialists all contradicted each other. Unless she had a pneumothorax, Olga would die; a pneumothorax was
certain death. She must be sent to a sanatorium, above all she must
not go to a santorium. Finally she was admitted to the Beaujon hospital and was given a pneumothorax. It was all the more heartrend-
ing because Dullin was about to revive *The Flies*. The project was
abandoned, for neither Dullin nor Sartre wanted anyone else for
Electra.

At Mégève, I had finished *All Men Are Mortal,* begun in 1943.
Back from America, Sartre read the last part of it in the noisy, smoky
cellar of the Méphisto, where we were spending most of our evenings
at that time.

"How can one consent to not being everything?" Georges Bataille asks in *L'Expérience Intérieure.* The phrase had struck me
because that had been Françoise's devouring hope in *She Came to
Stay:* she had wanted to be everything. I regretted not having shown
this illusion and its collapse in a clearer light, and decided to rework
that theme. Gnawed by ambition and envy, my new hero was to seek
complete identification with the universe and then discover that the
world resolves itself into individual liberties, each of which he is
unable to attain. While in *Blood of Others* Blomart believes himself
responsible for everything, this man would suffer the incapacity to do
anything. In this way, his story would be a complement to my first
novel and the antithesis of my second. But I didn't want it to re-
semble them. In 1943 and 1944, I had been obsessed by History, and
it was on the historical level that I meant to situate myself; not
content with possessing riches and fame, my hero would also seek to
influence the course of events. I had the idea of making him immortal; this would make his failure even more shattering. I set out to
explore in every direction what it would mean to be immortal. I
continued the meditation on death into which I had been drawn by
the war; I questioned myself about the meaning of time; it had been

brutally revealed to me, and I had realized that it was just as capable as space of dividing me from myself. I gave no answers to the questions I raised. *Blood of Others* had been conceived and constructed abstractly, but around the story of Fosca I let my dreams cluster.

The dominant theme, which reappears perhaps a little too stubbornly throughout the book, is the conflict of the point of view of death, of the absolute, of Sirius, with that of life, of the individual, of the earth; at twenty I was already vacillating, in my private notebooks, from one to the other; I had set them in opposition in *Pyrrhus et Cinéas;* in *She Came to Stay* what happens to Françoise is that, whether from wisdom or weariness, she renounces the world of the living and slides into the indifference of death; against the intolerable present, Hélène, in *Blood of Others,* tries to use the infinity of the future as an alibi; this time, too, I was confronting the relative and the absolute through History; but we had gained our victory, the present was all we could desire; it was the future that made us uneasy. We had disdained the grumbling voices which had whispered in August 1944: "And after?" and also the disaster mongers who prophesied in 1945: "The Third World War has just begun." I didn't imagine that the atom bomb was going to blow up the whole world the next day; nevertheless the meaning of the Allied victory had been compromised, and I wondered: What is the true substance of our present? Between the nihilism of the false prophets and the giddiness of the good-timers, where should we take our stand?

First of all I involved Fosca in a finite undertaking: the achievement of glory, at Carmona. In order to gain success, he chooses immortality; but this terrible privilege makes him aware of the counter-finalities that corrode and destroy all individual successes; the personal pride embodied by Fosca divides Italy and leaves it defenseless against the King of France, then against the Emperor of Austria. Then Fosca renounces his country and becomes the *éminence grise* of Charles the Fifth; if he could succeed, through the Emperor, in uniting the whole world, then his work would be proof, he thinks, against the challenges of time; but how make the whole world one when each man is unique? Terrified by the massacres and the misery brought about by the search for universal Good, he begins to doubt this Good itself; men reject, even at the price of terrible destruction, like the Anabaptists, that motionless fulfillment which would leave them nothing more to *do.* The universe is nowhere, he realizes: "There is nothing except men, men forever divided"; he renounces the idea of governing them: "There is nothing to be done for mankind; their good depends only on themselves. . . . They do not want happiness: they want to live. There is nothing one can do for them, there is nothing one can do against them. There is nothing one can do."

Fosca's unhappy experience covered the end of the Middle Ages and the beginning of the sixteenth century. Stupid wars, a chaotic economy, useless rebellions, futile massacres, population increases unaccompanied by any improvement in the standard of living, every thing in this period seemed to me confusion and marking time; I had chosen it for this very reason. The conception of history that emerges from this first part is resolutely pessimistic; I did not by any means consider it as cyclic, but I denied that there was any progress in its course. How could I think that my own epoch was any better than those before it, when it had so multiplied the honors of the past on battlefields, in concentration camps, in bombed cities? The romanticism and the moralism that counterbalance this pessimism also came from the circumstances of that time; our friends who had died in the Resistance, all the members of the Resistance who by their deaths had become our friends—all they had done had been of very little use, even of no use at all; one had to accept their lives as their own justification; one had to believe in the value of devotion, of ardor, of pride, of hope. I still do believe in those values. But does the separateness of men prevent humanity from undertaking any collective conquest? That is another question.

In any case, I did not say so. The somber vision proposed in the early part of the novel is challenged in the final chapter. The victories won by the working class since the beginning of the Industrial Revolution were another truth I recognized. In fact, I had no philosophy of history, nor does my novel arrive at one. In the triumphal march that closes his recollections, Fosca sees only the trampling of feet, but he does not hold the key to the enigma. First he had surveyed the world with the eye of a politician fascinated by its forms— city, nation, universe; next, he had given these forms a content —men; but he tried to govern them from outside, almost like a God; when he understands at last that they are free and self-determining, that one can serve but not possess them, he is too exhausted to feel any friendship for them; his defection does not deny History its meaning: it simply shows that the breaks between generations are necessary in order to move ahead. The Communists, following

Hegel, speak of Humanity and its future as of some monolithic individuality. I was attacking this illusion by embodying this myth of
unity in Fosca; the meanderings, the backslidings, the miseries of
History, and its crimes, are too hard to encompass for one consciousness to recall them down through the length of centuries without yielding to despair; fortunately, from father to son, life begins
afresh indefinitely. But this perpetual renovation implies also the
pain of separation. If the desires that inspired the men of the eigh-
teenth century are realized in the twentieth, the dead have no joy in
the harvest; Fosca, swept along in a tumultuous procession, thinks of
the woman he had loved a hundred years before: what is happening
now, he tells himself, is exactly what she wanted then, it is not at all
what she would have wanted now. This discovery completes his defeat. He cannot create a living link between the centuries, since they
transcend each other only by forswearing what they have been; if he
feels indifferent to the people who live in those centuries, there is
nothing to involve Fosca in their projects; if he loves them, he cannot bear the infidelity to which his destiny condemns him.

For Fosca represents the terrible pit of forgetfulness and betrayal;
I had experienced the cruel pain of being unable to grasp in any way
the deaths of others; all absences are contradicted by the immutable
plenitude of the world. In my second novel, Blomart thinks of a
friend killed at the age of twenty: "Who has he not been?"; about a
woman he loved, Fosca wonders: "Where is she not?" Several times I
put into his mouth a phrase that appears once in *The Mandarins* as
well: "The dead were dead, the living lived." He cannot even toy
with the hope that he will *always* remember; for him that word has
no meaning. All his dealings with humanity are perverted by this
fact; he never reaches the true meaning of friendship or love because
the whole basis of our brotherhood is that we all must die: only an
ephemeral being is capable of finding the absolute within time.
Beauty cannot exist for Fosca, nor any of the living values instituted
by human finitude. To look at the world is, for him, to lay it waste,
for he sees with the eye of God, whom I rejected at the age of fifteen,
the eye of the Being who transcends and levels everything, who
knows everything, who can do anything, and turns man into a worm.
From everyone he encounters, Fosca steals the world, without reciprocity; he casts them into the agonizing indifference of eternity.

That is Régine's tragedy, which I conceived as a counterpoint to
that of Fosca. An immortal being I could endow with the most far-

reaching ambitions, but not, since he has no peer, with that emotion of mingled fascination and rancor, human envy; I bestowed it instead on a woman greedy for domination over her fellow men and in revolt against all limitations—the glory of others and her own death. When she meets Fosca, she wants to inhabit his immortal heart; then she will become, she thinks, the Unique. What happens is the opposite; under his gaze, she crumbles; all her enterprises and her virtues conceal merely an absurd effort to exist, identical with the effort of all other men; with terror, she sees her life degraded to the status of a farce;[1] she sinks into madness. She had glimpsed a way to salvation, but lacked the strength to cling to it; she should have held fast to her own mortality. One of the main characters, Armand, meets Fosca face to face and is not turned to stone because he is committed body and soul to his own epoch. This morality relates to the conclusions of *Pyrrhus et Cinéas,* but it is not driven home in the form of a lesson; rather, it serves as a pretext for an imaginary experience. Some critics, the very ones who are annoyed when a novel *proves* something, blamed this one for not proving anything; which is precisely the reason why, despite the *longueurs,* the repetitions, the excesses, I still feel warmly toward it. Revealing it, I asked myself: But what was I trying to say? I was trying to say nothing more than the story I invented. The conflict is presented throughout within the narrative itself; an attempt to isolate specific assertions from it would only produce a set of contradictions; no one point of view finally prevails; Fosca's point of view and Armand's are true together. In my earlier essay I had said that the dimension of human enterprise is neither the finite nor the infinite but the indefinite: this word cannot be fixed within any given limits, the best way of approaching it is to explore its possible variations. *All Men Are Mortal* is an organized version of such an exploration; its themes are not theses, but points of departure for uncharted wanderings.

Once back from Tunisia, I had begun an essay in which I was tackling the same questions. I had had the idea for it a year earlier. In February 1945 I had given a lecture at Gabriel Marcel's to a group of mainly Catholic students; I had taken with me an ex-pupil of Sartre's, Misrahi, an Existentialist and a Zionist. He belonged to the Stern group; every time Gabriel Marcel attacked me, he would

---

[1] The party scene, where she becomes conscious of the farce, recalls the scene in *She Came to Stay* when Elisabeth, receiving the trio, gets the impression that she is taking part in a parody; but her disturbance was only psychological; with Régine, it has a metaphysical dimension.

fling himself forward to defend me, vehemently and pertinently: he had made himself thoroughly disliked. When it was over, I had a chat with him upstairs at the Flore; I told him that in my opinion it was possible to base a morality on *Being and Nothingness,* if one converted the vain desire to be into an assumption of existence. "You must write it!" he told me. During that winter, Camus had asked me, though I can't remember for what collection, for an essay on action; the reception of *Pyrrhus et Cinéas* was an encouragement to return to philosophy. Besides which, when I read Lefebvre, Naville or Mounin, I always wanted to reply. It was partly against them, therefore, that I undertook to write *The Ethics of Ambiguity.*

Of all my books, it is the one that irritates me the most today. The polemical part still seems valid. I was wasting time rebutting absurd objections; but at the time Existentialism was being treated as nihilist philosophy, willfully pessimistic, frivolous, licentious, despairing and ignoble; some defense had to be made. I commented critically and, to my mind, convincingly, on the delusion of the *one* monolithic humanity used by Communist writers—often without admitting it—in order to evade the difficulties presented by death and failure; I sketched the antinomies of action, man's indefinite transcendence against his demand for regeneration, the future against the present, the collective reality against the interiority of every being; returning to the question of ends and means, a burning one at the time, I demolished certain sophistries. On the role of the intellectual within a government he approves, I raised problems that are still topical today. And I still subscribe to the passage on estheticism, and to the reconciliation I suggested between the remote impartiality of the work of art and the commitment of the artist. The fact remains that on the whole I went to a great deal of trouble to present inaccurately a problem to which I then offered a solution quite as hollow as the Kantian maxims. My descriptions of the nihilist, the adventurer, the esthete, obviously influenced by those of Hegel, are even more arbitrary and abstract than his, since they are not even linked together by a historical development; the attitudes I examine are explained by objective conditions; I limited myself to isolating their moral significance to such an extent that my portraits are not situated on any level of reality. I was in error when I thought I could define a morality independent of a social context. I could write an historical novel without having a philosophy of history, but not construct a theory of action.

I had contributed four articles to *Les Temps Modernes* which were afterward published by Nagel as a book, of which three also deal with morals; so soon after a war which had forced us to re-examine all our ideas, it was natural enough to attempt to reinvent rules and reasons. France was crushed between two blocs, our fate was being decided without us; this state of passivity prevented us from taking practice as our law; I find nothing surprising, therefore, in my concern with moral questions. What I find hard to understand is the idealism that blemishes these essays. In reality, men defined themselves for me by their bodies, their needs, their work; I set no form, no value above the individual of flesh and blood. On my return from Portugal, when I blamed the English for their complicity with a regime condemned for one thing by its tragically high rate of infant mortality, Herbaud said to me: "Agreed, it's regrettable that there should be children dying of poverty; but perhaps that isn't too high a price to pay for the miracle of English democracy." I was revolted. I also quarreled with Aron, who thought England's higher interests justified the measures she was taking against immigration in Israel: the beauties of English democracy were so much hot air to these hopeless men jammed in the camps or on ships without harbor. But then, why did I take this circuitous route through other values besides need to justify the fundamental importance I assigned to need itself? Why did I write *concrete liberty* instead of *bread,* and subordinate the will to live to a search for the meaning of life? I never brought matters down to saying: People must eat because they are hungry. Yet that was what I thought. In *Oeil pour Oeil,* I justified the purges after the Liberation without ever using the one solid argument: these mercenaries, these murderers, these torturers must be killed, not to prove that man is free, but to make sure they don't do it again; for one Brice liquidated, how many lives would have been spared! I was—like Sartre—insufficiently liberated from the ideologies of my class; at the very moment I was rejecting them, I was still using their language to do so. That language has become hateful to me because, as I now know, to look for the reasons why one should not stamp on a man's face is to accept stamping on it.

After his return from America, Sartre talked to me a great deal about M. At present, their attachment was mutual, and they envisaged spending two or three months together every year. So be it:

separations held no terror for me. But he evoked the weeks he had
spent with her in New York with such gaiety that I grew uneasy; till
then I had supposed him to be attracted mainly by the romantic side
of this adventure; suddenly I wondered if M. was more important to
him than I was; my heart's old armor of optimism fell away; anything could happen to me. In a relationship that has lasted for fifteen
years, how much is a matter of mere habit? What concessions does it
imply? I knew my answer: not Sartre's. I understood him better than
I used to, and for that reason I found him more opaque; there were
great differences between us; this did not disturb me, quite the contrary, but him? According to his accounts, M. shared completely all
his reactions, his emotions, his irritations, his desires. When they
went out together, she always wanted to stop, to go on again, at
exactly the same moment he did. Perhaps this indicated a harmony
between them at a depth—at the very source of life, at the wellspring
where its very rhythm is established—at which Sartre and I did not
meet, and perhaps that harmony was more important to him than our
understanding. I wanted to free my heart of this uncertainty. It often
happens that when a dangerous question is burning our lips we
choose a particularly unsuitable moment to ask it. We were just
leaving my room to have lunch with the Salacrous when I asked:
"Frankly, who means the most to you, M. or me?" "M. means an
enormous amount to me, but I am with you." His answer took my
breath away. I understood it to mean: "I am respecting our pact,
don't ask more of me than that." Such a reply put the whole future
in question. It was all I could do to shake hands, to smile, to eat; I
saw that Sartre was watching me uneasily, I pulled myself together,
but I felt that the lunch would never be over. That afternoon, Sartre
explained what he had meant: we had always taken actions to be
more truthful than words, and that is why, instead of launching into
a long explanation, he had invoked the evidence of a simple fact. I
believed him.

Shortly after his return, Sartre caught the mumps. He retired to
his bed in the round room; a doctor painted his neck and his face
with black ointment. At the end of a few days he was able to receive
visits from friends. Not all of them came: his illness scared some off.
All the same, the room was always crowded and I had difficulty protecting him from bores.

During this time, I kept a diary. Here are some extracts from it;

they reveal what my memory cannot revive: the daily dust of my daily life.

April 30, 1946

When I went out at five this afternoon, the Carrefour de Buci was swarming with activity; women buying cauliflowers, asparagus, the first strawberries; they were selling slips of lily of the valley in little pots wrapped in silver paper. On the walls, the words YES and NO were scrawled in huge chalk letters.[1] Last year, there was something miraculous about spring, it was the first spring of the Liberation. This is already a peacetime spring. There is food in the shops, dates for example, and cloth and books; in the streets there are buses and taxis; a great change from May last year.

At *Les Temps Modernes,* I found Merleau-Ponty, Leiris and Ponge. Ponge has left *Action* (for what reason?). He says he finds having to choose between all the objects he'd like to describe perplexing: why not write for twenty years about moss? Or, from the opposite point of view, why not write about everything one encounters as one encounters it, without preference? He has more than two hundred poems still waiting to be finished, and expects to publish them someday in the form of an alphabet with illustrations. Gave Genet's and Laronde's poems to Festy to be printed, and told him I shall definitely not publish my novel in the magazine. Had a drink with Merleau-Ponty and Suzou at the Pont-Royal. Went home. With Sartre, still swathed in Velpeau bandages and wearing a pointed nightcap, I found Lefèvre-Pontalis. Sartre much better; brought him some books and magazines and made his dinner. Went to the Petit Saint-Benoît with Bost and Pontalis; Giacometti came in just as we did and sat with us. He was in better form than ever and told lots of stories. At the end of the meal, a saltcellar got knocked over. Bost picked it up; G. assumed his sorcerer's manner: "I wondered who would pick it up; and it was you!" "I wouldn't have picked it up," said Pontalis. "They always get picked up," said G. Then Bost: "Obviously, they're not meant to be upside down." Giacometti, appalled: "Ah! if you had said that in front of Breton, it would have been war!" He talked about the painter Christian Bérard: "He's so handsome!" "As handsome as Sartre?" I asked. He re-

[1] They referred to the referendum on the Constitution proposed by the Constituent Assembly and supported by the Communists.

plied, very seriously: "It's different. Sartre has a classical, Apollonian beauty; Bérard is Dionysiac." Finished the evening at Chéramy's.

This morning, Boubal approached me with a radiant smile. "If you read in the paper that M. Sartre is at death's door, don't get upset; there was a journalist looking for him, so I said: 'He's ill, it may be the end.' 'What's the matter with him?' 'A mysterious disease.' "

On the stairs, I ran into B.,[1] who was on his way up to see Sartre; I stopped him; he told me he knew a lot of bores were always trying to see Sartre and he didn't want to bore him, but he had something fascinating to tell him: a friend of his, Patrix, has brought off "a plastic transposition of the viscous." Apparently it's "a grandmother, an old grandmother who turns into a candle."

May 1st

Last year it was snowing, I remember. This morning was bright blue. Stayed in. Drank a cup of Nescafé and worked on *The Ethics of Ambiguity*. Sartre better; no more helmet of bandages, no more nightcap; instead, long black sideburns and a beard that looks like vegetation; he's still swollen, with a pimple on his nose. The dirty dishes, old papers, books, pile up day after day in his room; there's no place to put one's feet. He read me some Cocteau poems, very pretty. Outside there was bright sunlight: through the windows, one was very much aware of the street with its lily of the valley sellers and the peddlers selling stockings and rayon panties. I didn't put on stockings or coat to go out. Lilies of the valley everywhere, and all the chestnut trees along the Boulevard Pasteur heavy with white and red flowers, they're even beginning to lose their petals. Had lunch at my mother's; she's reading *Darkness at Noon*. Coming back, in the subway, I saw posters for Dullin's company with no mention of *The Flies;* that gave my heart a pang.

The first posters about the referendum are up on the hoardings: Vote YES, vote NO. All the *nos* have been crossed out.

Work. At six in the evening, had a drink with Bost and Rolland at the Bar Vert which is making a clumsy attempt to compete with Chéramy's; beautiful posters, but ugly red tables and aggressively green walls. Youki was there in a pretty black-and-white check dress; she talked about the Belgian poet she had sent to me at the magazine.

---

[1] An ex-pupil of Sartre's, who had become a doctor.

"You know," she said with her usual unawareness, "my house is the house of poets."

May 2nd

Even fairer and warmer than yesterday. Lilies of the valley everywhere; there are more flowers this spring than I can ever remember. Went with Bost to Beaujon. From a long way off you see the hospital, built of brick, with its great red crosses; it's very tall, grand and severe, and reminds me of Drancy. Lots of people in front of the main door, women mostly, dressed in their best clothes; one would think that these visits are a sort of holiday for them; they laugh among themselves in the elevator as it slowly climbs up the eleven floors. The eleventh floor is for chest patients; young women are on one side of the ward, older ones on the other; there's a single line of beds facing a large balcony with a grille (to prevent suicides, since some of the patients, especially the younger ones, would gladly throw themselves out of the window); there's a wide view of the suburbs, with a German prisoner-of-war camp in the foreground and, beyond that, the whole of Paris. Olga's room is a large, white cube which also opens onto this balcony. She says the view is extraordinarily beautiful in the evening, when all the lights come on. She's looking well today, hair carefully arranged, wearing makeup. She's had a third insufflation. She's now been in bed fifteen days and is beginning to get impatient.

In the bus, I read Troyat's *Life of Pushkin*, which I find interesting, and glanced through *Samedi-Soir*. There's a piece about *Arrival and Departure*. "Koestler brings great pathos to his understanding of the anxieties of our age but is unable to provide us with any means of escaping them." That's the kind of criticism that really goes far. I've heard at least a hundred discussions of the book; the fairest is what Giacometti said the other day: Roubachev ought to oppose No. 1 in the name of some other objectivity, not merely subjectivity; there should be some explicit issue between them, of a political or technical kind; without it Roubachev is unconvincing.

Work. Went to see Sartre at eight; he was reading *Prête-moi ta Plume* by Scipion, who today was awarded the prize for satire given by the newspaper *Le Clou*, and whose picture is all over *Combat*. He's seen Pontalis, who likes Bost's book very much;[1] and Genet,

---

[1] *Le Dernier des Métiers.*

who wanted Sartre to write a letter in his behalf asking the Minister for authorization to visit the reform schools. Bost is looking for a subject for a *Combat* article; I suggested one on the Hôtel Chaplain. He told us a lot about *Combat,* about the passion Pascal Pia was bringing to the task of killing the newspaper and himself with it, about Ollivier, whom everyone loathes and who knows it, about Aron, who's also getting himself disliked by understanding *Combat* so intensely and insisting on saying so. Everyone congratulated Bost on his article about the Pope, and Altmann came up from *Franc-Tireur* to say: "It's below the belt, but it's damned good." People were stunned by the conviction with which he called a surplice a bolero and a skullcap a caul. There have been three canceled subscriptions.

May 3rd

A morning of work in my room. In the afternoon, looked through the weeklies with Sartre. There are stories in *Cavalcade* and in *Fontaine* about the fact that we now go to the Pont-Royal instead of the Flore. A fairly friendly article by Wahl on Existentialism occasioned by Merleau-Ponty's lecture. Went over to the magazine. Lots of people there. Vivet introduced me to one of his friends: "X, who's enormously talented." I said to him: "I congratulate you; what do you have for us?" "Anything." A pause, then he asked: "What would you like?" "Anything." Another pause. "Well, thank you very much," he said. "No, I'm the one to thank you."

Paulhan has put together a very nice collection of texts: extracts from his own work, from Léautaud and from baroque manuscripts. I went to thank him. In his office, ten people dipping into a box. "We were looking at photos of all the places Rimbaud visited," Paulhan told me. "Would you like to have a look?" But I went to collect some proofs from Festy and then had a drink with the Leirises at the Pont-Royal. Met Roger Stéphane there, and he asked to have his "Conversation with Malraux" back.

Back at Sartre's we were talking once more about the connection between lucidity and liberty, and whether our moral system is not really an aristocratic one. Bost dropped in. He told us that there was a great to-do at *Combat* because of the recent articles by Ollivier and Aron championing the *No;* many of the people on the paper were going to vote *Yes;* and they wanted to start a campaign urging people to vote Socialist; otherwise *Combat* would become a right-wing paper. It appears that everyone stays on only because of Pia's personal charm, and he's so absorbed by his anti-Communism that he forgets he's supposed to be a leader of the Left.

Had an ice at the Flore while I read *la Médiation chez Hegel,* from which I learned nothing. Adamov was there, Henri Thomas, Marthe Robert, then Giacometti, Tzara and a host of others. I bought some tea at Boubal's and then went home to bed.

May 4th

A gray morning, rather cold. Went to the L.'s to get the Malraux interview for Stéphane. It puts Malraux in a very unsympathetic light; he thinks he's Goethe and Dostoyevsky rolled into one, and talks about everyone very maliciously. About Camus: "Oh please, let's be serious. We're not at the Café de Flore. Let us talk about La Bruyère or Chamfort." Stéphane says to him (I don't know where he got such an idea): "Sartre wants to write a big, sordid book about the Resistance." Malraux replies: "I shall write one that will not be sordid." But he defends himself pretty well against the accusation that he's becoming a Fascist: "When a man has written what I have written, he does not become a Fascist."

Work. From time to time, automobiles with loud speakers on them go by the window yelling: "Vote No!" or "Vote Yes!" One hears about nothing but the vote. We have no electoral registration card. (We went to the *mairie,* but didn't make a fuss.) Pouillon isn't going to vote, and Bost probably won't either, but we discuss it all the same. Besides, the result is a foregone conclusion; the public opinion poll this week showed a 54 percent *Yes* vote.

At half past twelve, Pontalis stopped by the hotel. He had met Genet the day before at Sartre's bedside and asked him: "Would you like a weed?" Genet looked him up and down. "Why do you call a cigarette a weed?" And he gave him a long lecture, explaining that culture, as Herriot put it, is what's left when one has forgotten everything, but that that was no excuse for going around pretending one had forgotten everything in order to seem cultured—as if that was Pontalis' main concern! Pontalis brought Sartre a hard-boiled egg and some ham, which he pulled out of his pocket with a somewhat shamefaced air. They had a long conversation; Sartre said we couldn't spend our lives thinking everything the Communist Party does is idiotic and help them at the same time; the best thing is to vote Communist and vote *No* to the referendum. Pontalis left, very shaken.

Found Pouillon and Bost at the Flore. Pouillon just back from Nuremberg; it's appalling, he says, to see how they all play the game, lawyers and defendants included; he's going to write a piece on it for *T.M.* He says that if he votes it will be *No,* because as recording secretary he was present at the drawing up of the Constitution and finds it despicable; but he won't vote; he'd have to go out to the country to do it. He justifies himself by saying: "M. Gay has announced that anyone who doesn't vote is a traitor and a malefactor; given what M. Gay is, one can only respect oneself by not voting."

To Beaujon with Bost. Olga doesn't seem too impatient.

Leaflets in the hotel corridors: VOTE No. Back in Sartre's room we decide that people, whether they vote *Yes* or *No,* will do so reluctantly. I said: "I'm keeping out." "It's very bad to say that!" Sartre told me. "But you're not voting yourself." "Voting isn't what's important; it's knowing which way you would vote." I had to laugh, as Giacometti would say.

Ate dinner at the Catalans with Bost; Solange Sicard was there, Grimaud, etc. Bost showed me a very friendly article about him by Vintenon, and Fauchery showered him with bouquets on the radio.

Sunday May 5th

When I've been working very hard, there are sometimes days when I feel like those dabfish which have used all their energy spawning and get washed up onto the rocks, dying and drained. Felt like that this morning. Had bad dreams which left a sort of chill around my heart. Blue sky, blustering wind; the newspaper vendors shouting very loud, some sort of argument going on in the *carrefour:* the referendum. We aren't voting, partly through fecklessness and laziness, because we haven't got voters' cards, and mainly because we probably would have abstained anyway.

Work. At four, went to see Palle and asked him to make some alterations in his article on Petiot. He was very tanned and handsome and very nice. He hasn't voted either.

Chéramy's in the evening; the radio gave the results of the referendum. To everyone's surprise there seemed to be a preponderance of *No's.* A great many abstentions. It's because people are just as uncomfortable about saying *Yes* as about saying *No.*

Went home, still feeling this strange anxiety around my heart. There must be people who feel like this most of the time, their skin separating them from the world; it must make a big difference to one's life. This evening everything was somehow tainted with horror: for example, the woman's hand I saw, all the bones showing so clearly, fingering its way through blond hair; the hair was a plant, with a *root* in the scalp. The word *root* was fascinating and frightening as I fell asleep.

Monday May 6th

Result of the referendum: *No* by 52 percent against 48 percent; 20 percent of the voters abstained. Ran out to get the papers immediately; no copies of *Humanité* or *Populaire* left; the Right is patting itself on the back, naturally.

Lunch at the Petit Saint-Benoît with Merleau-Ponty, who defended the Communist point of view; that led to Sartre's philosophy, which he thinks has an insufficient feeling for the dense intricacy of reality. This revived the desire to write my essay, but I'm too tired, I don't know why. Sartre is making a miraculous recovery; he shaved and put on a beautiful pair of new blue pajamas. Genet stopped by and left him the magnificent book Barbezat has printed, *Le Miracle de la Rose,* enormous, with huge black letters and red headings.

Went up to my room at four, and was so tired I slept for two whole hours. Then I set to work and suddenly my head was buzzing with ideas. At ten, went down to see Sartre. The room was very dark, with just the little lamp over his head switched on. Genet and Lucien were there. No one knows what's happened to the manuscript of *Pompes Funèbres* that was entrusted to Gallimard. Genet says he'll do something terrible if they've lost it.

Tuesday May 7th

Tea, newspapers, work. Sartre began his sketches of America,[1] which rather tire him. Genet stopped by to see me. He's just had a row with the Gallimards about the lost manuscript; he bawled them out and then he added: "And on top of all that, your employees think they can treat me like a faggot!" Claude Gallimard didn't know where to look. To Beaujon with Bost. They've given Olga a

[1] Which he abandoned.

final insufflation, and she'll know tomorrow whether it's taken or not. She had seen some young women in the X-ray room who had just been operated on and had bits of metal sticking out of them, and that has upset her terribly. She finds it hard to take all that bright, white light in her room, and also the windows onto the corridor which allow everyone to look in at her.

At the Flore, Montandon showed me a copy of *Labyrinthe* which contained an announcement about our lectures in Switzerland and some quite good pictures of Sartre and myself. Congratulated Dora Marr on her show, which I visited the day before yesterday. At Gallimard's I passed Chamson on the stairs; he asked after Sartre. "He's got mumps," I said. He began to back down the stairs away from me. "But that's contagious." "Very; I'm probably giving it to you this very moment." He fled. I frightened M., too, when he came in to bring me some rather uninteresting pieces on England. A visit from Ansermet; then one from a young man who wants to do some articles on the cinema, then a young couple who sing completely amoebic songs about their nights of love, then Rirette Nizan. She brought me a letter written by Nizan to his parents when he was seventeen; in it he recounts a conversation with Sartre in which they sat on the stairs and decided they were both supermen; then he elaborates all the moral considerations that follow from this fact. Went home. On the stairs I met a girl who said she was an ex-pupil of mine and then asked me, on behalf of the Gallup Institute, how I saw the future of France. I told her I didn't see it at all, which she seemed to find very profound. With Sartre, looked through the letters and manuscripts I brought back from *T.M.* There were two chapters by Louise Weiss; I made a note of one passage. During the exodus a Frenchwoman meets her ex-lover, Andlau, wearing a German uniform: *Andlau, handsome, intelligent and cynical as ever— why should he have changed?—said with a smile: It seems to me you need a bath. Blanche smells the contempt.* There was also the *Mémoires d'un Obscur*, the story of a private who had been a prisoner of war; we'll publish the chapter recounting his life on the farm. Poems, stories, reviews. A young "Existentialist" of seventeen sends us a poem which begins: "The empty tends toward the full."

A visit from Genet and Barbezat. The owner of the Flore gave me another tiny book by Jean Ferry, with a very nice dedication. It's called *Le Tigre Mondain* and I like it very much.

May 8th

Slight headache, but did quite a lot of work all the same. The second part's giving me trouble, but it's interesting to find out what my own thoughts are.

Sartre got up for the first time. We're going to have a drink at the Rhumerie Martiniquaise and have a talk about the magazine and Sartre's *La Morale*. Spent the evening with Bost in his room. Bost says Aron and Ollivier couldn't care less about the way people have to live, about their exhaustion, their hunger; the problem just doesn't exist for them. He told us that people living in the Hôtel Chaplain recognized themselves in his *Combat* article, though he signed it Jean Maury, and they're wild with anger. We talked about the Communists again. We'll vote for them; but it seems as impossible as ever to reach any kind of ideological agreement with them. Lengthy vaticinations. The problem of our relationship with them is crucial for us and they won't allow us to resolve it; it's a dead end.

May 9th

Am annoyed because as soon as I work for an hour or two I get a headache; yet the work's interesting. In the afternoon, I went out with Sartre; we went up to his mother's and he admired the room that will be his. In the evening at the Flore I caught sight of Limbour and asked him to give me some topical squibs. Zette was there with Leiris. Bost is in a terrible state because the Hôtel Chaplain business is getting worse; some men have been around to *Combat* looking for him so that they can knock his teeth out.

May 10th

Vitold came around to see Sartre. Discussion about the possibility of a tour of Italy and of a performance of *No Exit* in Switzerland; Vitold's hesitating because he has a film to make in June. Lunched with him at the Brasserie Lipp, then went back for Sartre. We sat on the terrace of the Deux Magots; it was a beautiful day. We patched together a copy of *The Victors* so that it could be given to Nagel to be typed. A great fuss at the magazine. Vittorini came to the office with Queneau and Mascolo; he seems very shy and speaks French badly. He expressed his regret that we'd been invited to Italy by Bompiani, who's a reactionary publisher; he said: "If you'd been invited by *my party,* you'd have been driven around by car; we took

Eluard everywhere." We decided to have an exchange of magazines; we'll see each other in Milan and get an Italian issue ready. There was quite a crowd suddenly; Gaston Gallimard arrived; I had put my nose in his door earlier and then fled, because I'd had to shake hands with Malraux and Roger Martin du Gard: the two of them always carry such a load of high seriousness around with them, and Gaston Gallimard's den seemed to be full of incense. Now he wanted to talk to me about Genet who's written him a very rude letter, after his scene with Claude. He practically apologized to me, and assured me that the manuscript wasn't lost. Had to talk to a lot of people. The lubricious young couple were there; the man had brought me a story; he asked me in his naïve, singsong voice: "Will Sartre give me his vote for the Prix de la Pléiade?" I settled some things with Renée Saurel,[1] looking splendid with her wind-blown hair, caught a glimpse of Leiris, and took Nathalie Sarraute's manuscript to Paulhan; he wrote the title and the author's name on it in his beautiful script; by some miracle he was alone. He showed me a lovely little Wols that he'd framed in a box with indirect lighting.

At seven I met Queneau and his wife at the Pont-Royal. Georges Blin was there and took me up on the subject of *Sexualité et Existentialisme*. He gave me the best pages of a review by Wahl that's to appear shortly. Wahl's critical approach to *Being and Nothingness* is analytical in a surprising way: "The first paragraph on page 62 is good, but the tenth line is weak"—that sort of thing. I drank two gin fizzes and was very animated. Our eighth issue is out, and people seem to think it's quite brilliant.

The hotel's been repainted; it gets prettier every day, and now there's a beautiful, brunette chambermaid, an ex-client who's fallen on hard times, and another blond one who rustles and bustles around all over the place. One might almost think one was in a brothel. The redhead I got on with so well has disappeared.

Saturday May 11th

I seem to be working at half speed; I'm tired; it's so annoying to have obstacles in one's head. Lunch at Lipp with Sartre and Pontalis. Dullin signed his books at Odette Lieutier's. Camille had decorated the bookshop with masks and photos and a lot of beautiful things; Dullin looked very handsome and seemed happy, surrounded by a

1 She was the secretary at *Les Temps Modernes* at the time.

crowd of admirers. There are a few flags in the streets in honor of V Day; it makes one rather sad.

I'd like to work, but sleep instead, my head bothering me. Went down to see Sartre at six. Nathalie Sarraute was there, hair beautifully waved and wearing a lovely bright-blue suit. She explained quite soberly that we act as if we were Kafka's Castle; in our records, each person has a number he doesn't know; we allow so many hours per year to one, so many hours to another, and it's impossible to get an extra hour even by throwing oneself under a bus. We manage to convince her, after endless arguing, that we like her. She admits, moreover, that in her eyes we are pure abstractions, and that she doesn't give a damn about our contingent, human individuals. It's still "a straw man." She told us about her article on Valéry, which will undoubtedly be very entertaining.

Dined with Bost at the Golfe-Juan. The Gallimards were there with Badel. The one-eyed Salvation Army man with the scar sold Jeanne Gallimard a Bible.

Sunday May 12th

No time for this diary. I scarcely manage to jot down the day's anecdotes. The sky is overcast and the chestnut flowers are beginning to drop.

Worked this morning, after I had gone to the Deux Magots to buy cigarettes and rolls for Sunday breakfast. At noon, I met Pagniez there; he had brought a very amusing article on the history of the Constituent Assembly. Lunch with Sartre at Lipp; Vitold stopped by to discuss plans for Switzerland and Italy. Coffee at the Montana. Work. Felt full of enthusiasm because, at last, my headache had gone. Started over from the very beginning; it's always the most exciting part, doing the second draft and seeing it take shape. At six, a meeting of *T.M.* in Sartre's room. His mother had made some fritters and I brought some cognac I had bought from the manager. Vian was there with his trumpet to keep him company, he was going on to play at the Point Gamma afterward; that's how he earns his living. His *Chronique du Menteur* was too facile, but funny. Paulhan was there, Pontalis, Vivet and his friend, who argued that you couldn't blame Steinbeck for having written *Drop the Bombs,* because his book was a failure. We thought of doing a study of American *engagé* writing: how Steinbeck, Dos Passos, Faulkner allowed themselves to be recruited into providing propaganda for the state. Roger Grenier came too, and, at half past seven, when it was all over, Bost, fresh as a daisy. The next three issues are crammed to bursting point.

Bost stayed with us. He told us Olga had been receiving visits from some of the young girls in the main ward; she had been very struck by the callous way they talked about their illness. When Olga mentioned that she had no "threads,"[1] one girl told her: "Oh! you'll get threads quick enough. The cutter comes round once a month. As long as he's not here, you won't get any threads; but as soon as he does come back, you'll see, your threads will be down again." They told her that men suffer from T.B. much worse than women. Some of the girls lean out over the grille round the balcony, although it's very high and curves inward at the top. A great deal of flirting goes on between the eleventh floor and the men on the tenth. Often there are shows which everyone attends in pajamas. The tubercular patients despise the ones who aren't; they judge each other according to the seriousness of their cases and their moral resistance.

May 13th

For a long moment, I thought: "I am imprisoned inside my dream, the way it is in Henry's drawing; I'll never be able to get back into my room." There was a high fence all around my bed. At last I woke up, but it was already late, almost nine o'clock. I was in very good spirits because I'm not tired any more, and because Sartre is better and we're off to Switzerland on Saturday. Rolland has invited us to Constance. He said: "We'll be among friends—Hervé and Courtade will be there." No trace of irony in his voice: written insults don't count.

We had lunch at the Casque with Giacometti.

We're wondering how Breton will be received when he comes back to Paris. Aragon was stunned by the lack of enthusiasm which greeted *Personne ne m'Aime;* he thinks it was a fascist plot.

At the Flore I found three big handsome American books in which we'll choose the Wright texts for the August-September issue.

Work from three to six. Went to the Flore to settle things with Montandon about the Swiss trip. Glimpsed Salacrou with Sophie Desmarets, very beautiful with her red hair. Have come home to bring this diary up to date. I notice as I reread bits here and there that already it evokes nothing for me. And why should one hope that

---

1 A colloquial expression for adhesions.—Tr.

these words would be different from any others, that they should have the magic power of retaining life within themselves and re-suscitating the past? No. For myself, the last fifteen days are already merely sentences written down, nothing more. The only alternative would be to pay real attention to how one writes things down, and I haven't time.

Dined with Bost in Sartre's room; eggs and corned beef. Bost has been back to the Hôtel Chaplain and resumed diplomatic relations with Jeannette, who's relented slightly. He saw Wright on the ter-race of the Flore this morning and Wright laughed in his face; ap-parently he always laughs, but it's his way of avoiding contact with people. Sartre and Bost took turns in parting their hair in the middle to prove that it makes you look stupid. The main effect was to make them look more feminine, which is odd. Bost talked about the 70,000 word pulp books he used to write two years ago; he would write them in two days for 1,500 francs; one of them was called *Eva Was Only Beautiful*. He showed us a letter from a certain Jules Roy congratulating him; and another from a man complaining that the information signs in the *mairie* of the 16th Arrondissement are badly placed; his book is very successful. At eleven, Sartre's eyes began to get inflamed, though not without some encouragement, and we let him go to sleep. Had a drink at Chéramy's, where a mysterious gen-eral bought us a second. Bost talked to me about my novel which he finally took around to Gallimard today; he likes the Indian episode very much, but finds the beginning a bit drawn out. Pontalis also thinks it sounds too much like a chronicle.

Home at midnight and spent an hour rereading and continuing this diary. I'd like to take more trouble over it. Feel very comfortable in bed, nodding slightly between words. I can hear the rain falling gently outside, and footsteps a long way off. Tomorrow I'll work and soon I'll be going to Switzerland. I'm very happy with things as they are. At the moment, I'd really like to have a lot of time for writing.

Tuesday May 14th

Everything gray when I awoke. Thought about all the arrange-ments I've got to make; hate making arrangements, and hate think-ing about making them even more; especially since the more I think the less I actually do about them. Went out for the newspapers.

There was a malicious article by someone called Pingaud[1] about Bost's novel; Bost is obviously an Existentialist, this person writes, because he's dedicated his book to the Russian woman at the Café de Flore; and besides, Sartre published a great eulogy of the documentary novel in the first issue of *T.M.*, the same issue in which *Le Dernier des Métiers* first appeared. Another unfriendly article by little Clément on Existentialism. Found the manuscript of *Blood of Others* in a cupboard; I'm going to give it to Adamov for the Artaud benefit sale; it's a lovely manuscript, all dog-eared and covered with crossouts, and written on different sizes of paper with different inks and even in different scripts. It's so much more alive than a book; it makes you feel it really came from inside you; the memory of certain times when I was writing it still cling to it. Went through *Black Metropolis* to choose some things that might fit into our American issue. Wish I had more time to read.

Made some of my travel arrangements. Worked at the Pont-Royal. Went up to the office of *T.M.* at half past five. Alquié and Pouillon were discussing Communist policy with Sartre.

Aron stopped by for a moment; Paul Morihien came in to collect the *Anti-Semite and Jew* and my four articles from *T.M.* Went back down to the Pont-Royal to see Vian, who had brought me his novel and an American book on jazz from which we'll translate a piece. He told me that there are some very good radio plays in America, a bit naïve but charming, like the one about the little caterpillar who dances to "Yes sir, that's my baby," or the one about the little boy searching among the stars for his dog that's been run over by a bus, and then at the end you realize that the little boy's been run over too. He's going to write an article about them. His novel[2] is very entertaining, especially the lecture by Jean-Sol Partre, and the murder with the heart extractor. I also like Gouffé's recipe: "Take a small salami; skin it and ignore its cries."

Came home at eight with Sartre, who was very tired. The evening was very beautiful just then, the trees still wet, the red and green lights, a few lighted windows, and some of the day still left in the sky.

We ate some ham while going through the booty accumulated at the office. Some short stories, all bad; a very good "Nuremberg

1 Bernard Pingaud; he has since become our friend, and is on the board of *Les Temps Modernes.*
2 *L'Écume des Jours.*

Trial" by Pouillon; a good *Petiot* by Palle; Ponge's piece, *Ad Litem,* doesn't amount to much. A visit from Bost. Olga has her threads; she doesn't think they're taking proper care of her at the hospital; she must get out of there. He told us that there had been a riot in an American prison the day before, and five prisoners had been killed, but when he went to ask the U.S. information services about it, the officials angrily denied it.

In a lecture given at the Sorbonne to commemorate the anniversary of Descartes, Thorez has rehabilitated Descartes as a great materialist philosopher.

May 15th

Had to wait two hours at the Swiss Legation. But they passed quickly because I was reading Vian's *L'Écume des Jours,* which I like very much, especially the sad story of Chloé who dies with a water lily in her lung; he has created a world entirely his own, which is rare and always moving. The last two pages are electrifying; the dialogue with the Crucifix is the equivalent of the *"No"* in Camus' *Cross Purposes,* but less obvious and more convincing. What strikes me most is the truth of the novel, and also its enormous tenderness.

Lunch and coffee with Sartre at Lipp, at the Flore and at Chéramy's. Bought a lovely Blue Guide for Switzerland; it makes me excited and depressed at the same time, because I know there are so many things to see and I won't be able to see them. I'm afraid the trip is going to be rather official. But I look forward to it all the same.

On the stairs, a lanky young man with an umbrella came up to me and asked what Sartre meant by "essence." I referred him to *Being and Nothingness.* He told me that he had read it of course, but he didn't want to be superficial and so I really ought to give him a definition in as few words as possible. It was for a newspaper in Strasbourg.

Thursday May 16th

Spring is coming back. On my way to buy some cigarettes, I saw some magnificent bunches of asparagus with the bottoms wrapped in red paper, lying on a green paper in a vegetable stall; they were so pretty. Work. I've rarely taken so much pleasure in writing as I do these days, especially in the afternoon when I come back at half past four into this room that's still thick with smoke from the morning, the paper already covered with green ink lying on the desk; and my cigarette and fountain pen feel so pleasant in my fingers. I can understand Duchamp's saying to Bost, when he asked him if he didn't sometimes regret not painting any more: "I miss the feeling of the tube of paint in my hand when I squeezed it and the paint smeared across the palette; that was nice." The physical part of writing is very pleasant. And even inside, I sense things loosening up; perhaps I imagine it. At any rate, I feel lots of things to say. There's also the idea for a novel that began to come to me yesterday, at Chéramy's.

The Kermadec show. Dinner at the Catalans with Sartre and Bost who shamelessly talk about New York in front of me.

May 17th

At the Flore with Sartre, at noon, I was introduced to Soupault. I still find it odd when I meet a man I admired from afar when I was twenty, and he turns out to be just a flesh-and-blood person, and getting on in years. Soupault asked me if I'd like to go to America. He promised to get me an invitation in October if I really want to go, and he amuses Sartre because he seems to be a bit concerned about my fragility. Of course I want to go, and I insisted, and I'm bursting to go, and yet at the same time I feel a mild pang at the thought of going away for four months.

This morning, in *Cavalcade,* there was a stupid and venomous article on Sartre by Monnerot. Also accounts of Mounin's article which is supposed to have K.O.'d Sartre; they're not hard to please. In *Littéraire,* there was an interview with students of the École Normale Supérieure by Paul Guth, in which Sartre was mentioned. And in the middle of an article by Billy on "literature and metaphysics" there was a drawing of me, very fat and bovine. Lunch at the Golfe-Juan with Pagniez and his wife. Pagniez defended reformism.

At *T.M.* we're setting up the ninth issue. It's astonishing the number of texts we have to choose from these days. People stopped by but didn't stay, and we were able to work in peace. It seems that Nero is out of prison, according to Merleau-Ponty. We had a drink at the Pont-Royal with Leiris, Queneau, their wives and Giacometti. Dinner at the Golfe-Juan with Giacometti and Bost. There was a long discussion about the trial of a gentleman farmer who recently took a gun and shot his gardener, who was his daughter's lover. The girl was sixteen, and the letters she wrote were so obscene they couldn't be read out in court; the gardener was thirty-six and an old offender; the father went with his son to keep watch in the girl's room, and they killed the gardener; the son missed the fellow twice, but the father got him. He's been condemned to only four years in prison, and the son got three years with a suspended sentence. Sartre made Bost laugh until he cried by developing the theory that the crime was a direct consequence of the last elections, that since the Liberation the father had felt surrounded by a revolting world and that this murder expressed the paroxysm of his revolt. Which led Giacometti to tell the story of Sergeant Bertrand, who was such a gentle, steady fellow, but every night went digging up corpses in cemeteries, cutting them up and nibbling the pieces; they could only punish him for desecration of graves, since neither the mutilation nor the ingestion of corpses had been provided for in the criminal code. He talked about Picasso, whom he had seen the evening before and who had shown him some drawings; it appears that, confronted with each new work, he's like an adolescent who has scarcely begun to discover the resources of art. He says: "I think I'm beginning to understand something; for the first time I've done some drawings that are really drawings." And he was delighted when G. said: "Yes, you're making progress." We finished the evening at Chéramy's. But, as I agreed with Bost, a diary is useless for this sort of thing; to keep any sort of record of the irresistible conversation between Sartre and Giacometti we needed a tape recorder.

May 18th

This evening I leave for Switzerland. For three weeks now I've scarcely left my room and seen almost no one except Sartre and Bost. It was restful and fruitful. This afternoon I'm upstairs at the Flore, near the window; I can see the wet street, the plane tree swaying in the sharp wind; there are a lot of people, and downstairs there's a great hubbub. I don't feel at ease here. Something tells me that I'll never again work here as I used to for so many years.

Bost came to look for me. He had received a short letter from Gide congratulating him on *Le Dernier des Métiers*. He also showed me an issue of *La Rue*, a newspaper that's being started by Jules Vallès but won't be out for a while; they're issuing just one number "to preserve the title." Prévert is in it, and Nadeau, some of Henry's drawings, and a lament by Queneau on the refrain *"Je suis un pauvre con."* We went to Beaujon. Olga told us about the patients she's seen. Yesterday, a young woman, mother of three children, went in to have a pneumothorax, they tried it three times in three different places, and three times it didn't work; in the end she fainted from sheer despair and remained unconscious for three-quarters of an hour. A little country girl was brought in, thinking she had only one lung affected; when she said to Dr. Benda, who had just looked at her X-ray: "I've come to have my pneumothorax," he asked her: "Which lung?" And that was how she found out that both her lungs were diseased. Olga says the worst part of it is that you gradually grow resigned to it as you lose your vitality.

Took the train for Lausanne. We were alone in the compartment except for a little, dark-haired girl who held her overnight bag pressed against her heart all night long; she slept sitting up. I stretched out and slept quite well. I can remember going to Limousin on the train when I was thirteen or fourteen and spending the whole night with my face at the window, swallowing soot and feeling immeasurably superior to all the grown-ups dozing in the warmth of the compartment. It's things like that that make me realize I've aged. Just for one moment there was a beautiful, bright moon in a sky streaked with clouds; and, in the morning, the mountains in a grayish-pink dawn. That still never fails, the shock of awakening, when I've been asleep for a long time and then suddenly I find I've been transported into an early morning somewhere a long way off. This feeling was strongest in the desert, before Tozeur; and then arriving at Sallanches in winter; and also, I don't quite know why, the wet countryside of Auvergne when I got to Mauriac.

Skira, the publisher who organized this lecture tour, had booked us in a hotel close to the lake in Geneva. From my window, I saw glistening swans and magnificent beds of flowers. Switzerland's opulence left me openmouthed. "It's one of the pleasantest and most forgotten things, being able to eat anything you like at any time," I noted; and again, later: "What a pleasure it is to be able to have supper after the cinema: it reminds one of before the war!" At the Brasserie du Globe, you could order as much whisky, sherry, port flips, or anything you felt like; there were little cards that said: TOAST AND RUSSIAN CAVIAR. I remembered going through Annemasse in

1943 and the emotion I felt when I saw a signpost that said: GENEVA, 9 KILOMETERS; and the people there said, in voices full of wonder: "At night, you can see the lights"; I saw the Kursaal with its illuminations, and the flashing of the neon signs. At Lausanne we were taken to a store that sold clothes "by correspondence and by temperament"; Sartre came away with a suit and a raincoat, and I with a green tussore silk dress and a red, white and blue linen skirt. In Geneva I had already bought some superb leather shoes, suitcases, and a watch with a black dial and green hands.

The three weeks were full of chores: not only the lectures themselves but book-signing sessions and radio interviews. One morning, we were accompanied by a camera for almost two hours through the somnolent streets of the old town; then there were the dinners, the receptions, the small talk. We got on very well with Skira and his pretty wife; he knew the surrealists, he had published them. "I was the lion tamer," he said. Detached almost to the point of absence and yet always disturbed, passionately interested in women, doubtless bursting with complexes for all his air of being a pleasure-seeking egotist, Albert Skira's conversation was cynical and very funny when he managed to relax. We got along well with Montandon, who ran *Labyrinthe,* too; we understood each other, despite his reservations about Existentialism: he belonged to the Labor Party and was a Marxist. "All the Swiss intellectuals are reactionaries," he told us. "During the war, there was an attempt to organize an anti-Nazi demonstration, and we could only find two old professors to take part. That's what persuaded me to become an out-and-out member of a working-class party." We met a few other people who were interesting and pleasant. But there were also a great many we were forced to see who bored or even repelled us.

Our first meal at the Globe overwhelmed me: "A magnificent meal, with tournedos, ices and very good Swiss wines; but horribly dreary. B.[1] is loathsome when he talks about the Arab midwives with whom he traveled by truck in Africa; they were encamped away from the others at night, 'because they smelled so badly'; they had been converted to Catholicism and protested in the name of their religion: 'But we have souls the same as you.' We just laughed at them, said B.; he told the story with intolerable complacency, and boasted extravagantly of his anti-Vichyism: 'I'm a *Vichyssois,* but not a *Vichyiste.'*

[1] A very high-ranking French official.

There was only one interesting moment, when Montandon described Merleau-Ponty's argument with Tzara about *Arrival and Departure*. Tzara insisted that Koestler was a bastard; his proof of this was the fact that, during the war, Koestler had been able to pay for his in-valid wife's stay in a sanatorium. At that Merleau-Ponty smashed a glass, saying: 'Under these conditions, no discussion is possible.' The gesture astonished me, especially since Merleau-Ponty could quite easily have reduced Tzara to a pulp; in any case, it was a healthy reaction. I was relieved when lunch was over. I find this sort of thing even more painful when I am with Sartre. Alone, as in Portugal or Tunis, it's bad enough, but when he's there I always think how much we could employ the time together, without the others. . . ."

The day after our arrival, we went for a walk in the environs of Interlaken; when we came back, Sartre received the press. When I came down into the lobby, there were already a lot of people around Sartre: a whole swarm of journalists, mostly old and frightfully proper. We went into the room off the lobby and found ourselves enthroned, side by side, like a Catholic king and his queen; I thought we looked rather ridiculous, especially me. A little old man with a white moustache opened fire; he hadn't read anything about Exis-tentialism, he said, he only knew about it from hearsay: "But it appears that it is a doctrine which permits everything; isn't that dangerous?" Sartre explained. The atmosphere was clearly hostile. In particular, there was a paunchy gentleman with squinting, wrinkled eyelids who paraded all the disabused, "realistic" superiority that re-actionary idealists tend to have; he questioned Sartre on education: "Should we respect the child's freedom?" And there was an assump-tion in the question that the worker is a child. (The questioner turned out to be Gillouin, Pétain's *éminence grise,* as we learned later from the press attaché, who was furious that he had managed to insinuate himself into the conference. The session lasted for more than an hour, with the help of a little vermouth and some cheese and biscuits. A dark-haired girl, with a braid, asked some questions with sympathy; all the others reeked of Fascism or religion, and were resolutely against us without knowing even what we were talking about.

I didn't go to Sartre's first lecture because I was out sight-seeing, but he told me about it. There were 1,100 people; they listened well but didn't clap much; he spoke for two hours. After that he drank four martinis, ate dinner and spent the evening dancing; naturally he didn't remember very much, except that he gave some advice to a very respectable lady from La Chaux-de-Fonds concerning her son's sex life. The lady was terrified he would get some tramp of a girl pregnant. "Then teach him to withdraw, Madame," Sartre told her. "Yes, of course," she said. "I'll tell him the advice came from you; it'll have more effect then."

In Zurich, Sartre gave a lecture, and there was also a performance of *No Exit* at the theater.

Wednesday

Skira came to pick us up at the station buffet, dressed in an amazing striped shirt and escorted by two men from the French bookshop, one sedate with dark hair[1] and the other lively and blond; both were very nice; they had made a display in the bookshop window from newspaper cuttings, books and caricatures and photographs of Sartre. *Labyrinthe* had covered the town with posters shouting Sartre's name in huge red letters. Dinner and a lecture. Sartre was greeted with applause on his entrance, and took off his overcoat like a boxer entering the ring: there were about six hundred people, mostly young, who seemed very interested. At six o'clock, the people at the bookstore had managed to send the journalists to meet the wrong train, but by now they'd found their way back and there were at least fifteen at our table, battering Sartre with questions. All this while, the dark-haired man from the bookstore was talking to me in his slow sad voice; he told me he had been a Communist, but then he'd become disgusted by the Party's methods. We talked a bit about Koestler: it's amazing how one always seems to find one's way back to the same conversations. . . .

Thursday

I met Sartre about seven, when he came back from rehearsal; he had terrified everyone by falling into an orchestra pit ten feet deep; there was a tarpaulin stretched over it; he walked on it, the cloth ripped, and he disappeared before their very eyes. "Good-bye lecture!" said the owner of the bookstore; then a rather dazed-looking face reappeared through the hole. We went to the theater. Full

1 This was Harold, who has since become known for his photographic montages.

house. I had a seat in the second row. Sartre spoke very well for twenty minutes about the theater; everyone seemed pleased. After rather a long wait, the curtain rose. The actors were a bit nervous. Chauffard had the shakes. Balachova was wearing a different wig and dress, an improvement on the old ones. They all fluffed their lines a bit, and the curtain didn't come down at the end; but they acted very well and there was a great deal of applause. We all went to supper in a big *brasserie* decorated with magnificent paintings by Picasso, Chirico, etc. They belonged to someone who was exhibiting his collection there. At midnight we split up. Sartre took Wanda home.[1] I left with Chauffard, and we had a gin fizz in a basement café; he was happy because Laffont was publishing his short stories. Didn't want to sleep at all; but they turned us out; after midnight, everything in Zurich closes. Outside, it was raining, and we were about to go our separate ways rather dolefully, when we met the bookstore man trudging along under a big umbrella. He suggested buying a bottle of wine and drinking it in the bookstore. We stayed there until three in the morning, looking at art books, drawings, magazines; Chauffard read aloud some obscene poems, signed Claudinet, which I thought might be by Cocteau[2]; the title of the book on the cover was *Vies*, but inside it was called *Vits*[3]; there was one very lovely one with the refrain: "If I had only had a couple of francs."

In Berne, we dined at the embassy; a theologian took me up at great length on nothingness, being, being-in-itself and being-for-itself. In Paris all conversations seemed to become political ones; in Switzerland they become theological. They even pressed Sartre very insistently with questions about the nature of angels. Existentialism had caused a quarrel between Ansermet and René Leibowitz; Ansermet wanted to reach an understanding of all music from the standpoint of Existentialism; but according to Leibowitz, only serial music can be considered in accordance with this philosophy. They had been insulting each other with great vivacity in *Labyrinthe*.

I gave a lecture at Lausanne. A lady came up to me as I was leaving. "I don't understand. M. Sartre talked so well! He looks so respectable! And yet it seems he writes the most dreadful things! But why, Madame? Why!" I also gave a talk to some students in Geneva. That night and the night after we went out with Skira and Annette,

---

1 Marie Olivier, the actress.
2 They are not, I have discovered.
3 The oral pun is on the French words for *life* and *penis.*—Tr.

a young woman in whom Giacometti was intensely interested.[1] We both thought her very attractive. To me, she seemed quite like Lise in many ways; she had the same dogged materialism, the same fearlessness, the same avidity; she devoured the world with her eyes; she didn't want to miss anything or anyone; she enjoyed violence and laughed about everything.

At a party in Lausanne, Sartre had met a young man, called Gorz, who knew all his writings like the back of his hand and talked very knowledgeably about them. In Geneva we saw him again. Taking *Being and Nothingness* as his starting point, he could not see how one choice could justifiably be given preference over another and consequently Sartre's commitment troubled him. "That's because you're Swiss," Sartre told him. As a matter of fact, he was an Austrian Jew who had settled in Switzerland since the war.

We saw Fribourg, Neuchâtel, Basel, and their museums. The villages were a bit too scrubbed and polished, but some of them were pretty. We drank white wine in *weinstübe* with spotless floors. We fell in love with the little squares and fountains of Lucerne, its painted houses, its towers and, above all, its two covered wooden bridges decorated with old painted pictures. We climbed up to Selisberg, where Sartre had spent vacations when he was little; he showed me his hotel, his room, with a balcony that stuck out over the lake: the balcony from which Estelle, in *No Exit*, throws her baby into the water. It rained a lot; I didn't care much for the fat Swiss women, or for the men with their velour hats bristling with edelweiss, or for the accordions and the songs they sang rather badly in chorus; but my mania still had me in its grip, and often I would leave Sartre in one of the towns and go up into the mountains for a few hours or a few days. I persuaded·him to go to Zermatt, and we rode in the funicular to the top of the Gonergratt, more than 9,000 feet up; sitting on a bench, our feet in the snow, we gazed for a long time at the Matterhorn, half hidden, like some fearful divinity, in its own private cloud. The next morning, we both felt as though our heads were screwed in a vice: mountain sickness. On the hotel terrace, there were sixty Swiss men, each with a badge in his buttonhole, examining the landscape with a knowledgeable air; they called themselves "the contemporaries of La Chaux-de-Fonds": contemporary with whom? We caught the train back to Paris. At Vallorbe, one of the customs officers said to Sartre, as he handed back his passport: "Your

1 She is now his wife.

books are unobtainable, Monsieur"; and then to me: "Still riding tandem?"

On his return from America, Sartre had received a letter from a *khâgneux*,[1] Jean Cau, asking help in finding work; he was preparing for the École Normale entrance exams, though this was his first attempt and he hadn't much hope; after the exams his parents would insist that he go back to live with them in the country. Sartre replied that he would look around for him. He fell ill, went to Switzerland, and didn't look around. In June, Cau—who had addressed similar requests to other writers without success—came to see him; the academic year was almost over. "All right," said Sartre, "be my secretary." Cau accepted. Sartre summoned him to the Deux Magots; but his mail had not yet become very voluminous; he didn't really need help with it. I can still see him, from my vantage point at a nearby table where I was working, hunting through his pockets and rooting out two or three meager envelopes; he explained to Cau what he should write in reply. He confided to me with a sigh that his secretary was in fact using up time instead of saving it. Cau found the situation irritating too; he had wanted employment, not charity. But the situation gradually improved when Sartre moved into the new apartment in the Rue Bonaparte with his mother. In the morning Cau would sit in the room adjoining Sartre's study, answering the telephone, making appointments and keeping the correspondence up to date; it seemed almost as though the organ had created the function. It was time that Sartre put some order into his life; but I wondered with some regret if he wasn't going to lose the liberty so dear to our youth.

The June issue of *Les Temps Modernes* appeared with the rubric: edited by Jean-Paul Sartre. The committee had fallen apart. Ollivier was moving toward the right; he sympathized with the Gaullist Union which had just come into being. Aron's anti-Communism was becoming more pronounced. At about that time, or a little later, we had lunch at the Golfe-Juan with Aron and Pia, who was also being attracted by Gaullism. Aron said that he had no great affection for either the U.S.A. or the U.S.S.R., but that if there were a war he would be on the side of the West; Sartre replied that he himself had no relish for either Stalinism or America, but that if war broke out he would be found in the ranks of the Communists. "In short,"

[1] Someone who "crams" *lycée* students for exams.

concluded Aron, "we should make different choices between the two evils; but in any case we should both be making the choice over our dead bodies." We felt he went too far in thus minimizing an antagonism we regarded as fundamental. Pia explained the Gaullist economic theory to us without so much as mentioning the problems of wages, of prices, of the working-class standard of living; I expressed my astonishment. "Oh! We'll leave all that Social Welfare business to the Jocistes," he answered contemptuously. In less than two years, the words Right and Left had resumed their old meanings, and the Right was gaining ground; in May the M.R.P. had gained a majority vote.

Genet told me about the *Dame à la Licorne* and I went to see the exhibition of French tapestry. *Citizen Kane* was finally shown in Paris: yes, Orson Welles had revolutionized the cinema. For the Prix de la Pléiade, Queneau and Sartre supported Boris Vian, but the jury chose Malraux's candidate, the Abbé Grosjean, instead.

My essay was finished, and I was asking myself: What now? I sat in the Deux Magots and gazed at the blank sheet of paper in front of me. I felt the need to write in my fingertips, and the taste of the words in my throat, but I didn't know where to start, or what. "How wild you look!" Giacometti said to me at one point. "It's because I want to write and I don't know what." "Write anything." In fact, I wanted to write about myself. I liked Leiris' *L'Age d'homme;*[1] such sacrificial essays, in which the author strips himself bare without excuses, appealed to me. I let the idea begin to take shape, made a few notes, and talked to Sartre about it. I realized that the first question to come up was: What has it meant to me to be a woman? At first I thought I could dispose of that pretty quickly. I had never had any feeling of inferiority, no one had ever said to me: "You think that way because you're a woman"; my femininity had never been irksome to me in any way. "For me," I said to Sartre, "you might almost say it just hasn't counted." "All the same, you weren't brought up in the same way as a boy would have been; you should look into it further." I looked, and it was a revelation: this world was a masculine world, my childhood had been nourished by myths forged by men, and I hadn't reacted to them in at all the same way I should have done if I had been a boy. I was so interested in this discovery that I abandoned my project for a personal confession in order to give all my attention to finding out about the condition of

[1] Published in America as *Manhood* in 1963.

woman in its broadest terms. I went to the Bibliothèque Nationale to do some reading, and what I studied were the myths of femininity.

On July 2nd, the Americans exploded a new bomb on Bikini. Personally, I was not—and have never been—much affected by the dangers of the atomic bomb; but many people were very alarmed. When Jean Nocher announced during a radio program that a chain reaction had accidentally been started, that matter was beginning to disintegrate, and that within a few hours we should all be dead, people believed him. "I was with my father," Mouloudji told me. "We went out for a walk, and we thought, It's the end of the world; we were very, very sad."

Our publisher, Bompiani, had invited us to Milan, and Mme Marzoli, who ran the big French bookstore in the city, had organized—in collaboration with Vittorini—one or two lectures for us. To see Italy again! The thought drove everything else from my mind. Circumstances were not propitious; Brigua and Tenda had just been assigned to France, and Italy was reproaching her "Latin sister" bitterly for this "stab in the back." Further, Tito was demanding that Trieste be ceded to Yugoslavia; and the French Communist intellectuals had signed a manifesto in support of his claim. Two days before the date fixed for our departure, I happened to be in the bar of the Pont-Royal; I was called to the telephone. It was Mme Marzoli calling me from Milan; she advised me to postpone our trip; the Italians were in no mood to listen to us. She was so insistent that if it had been Sartre on my end of the line, he would certainly have given in to her; I stubbornly refused to. It doesn't matter, we'll just keep quiet, I told her; but we've got a few lire at Bompiani's, we've got visas; we'll come anyway. She tried to dissuade me, but it was so much wasted breath; as I hung up I said: "See you soon!" I gave Sartre an expurgated account of the incident, for I feared his scruples.

We were welcomed when we arrived in Milan by the staff of the *Politecnico,* edited by Vittorini; our magazines were very similar; the first issues had both appeared at about the same time; a weekly at first, then a monthly, *Politecnico* had published Sartre's manifesto on *littérature engagée.* We had met Vittorini in Paris; I had read his *Conversations in Sicily* in French. He was fanatically attached to his Party. "If you cut me into eighty pieces, you'd end up with eighty little Communists," he used to say; yet we felt no barrier between us.

From the very first evening, dining to the sound of a violin in the Milanese intellectuals' favorite restaurant, with Vittorini himself and his friends—Vigorelli, Veneziani, Fortini and a few others—we realized that in Italy the Left presented a solid front. We talked late into the night. Vittorini told us about the difficulties the Italian Communists had just encountered. First of all, in the name of Revolutionary Internationalism, they had supported Tito; but the reactions of the rank and file had convinced them to switch to the patriotic gambit, and now they were singing the same tune as the rest of the country. He told us that Eluard, who was in Italy on a lecture tour, had warmly supported their original policy and given it his endorsement in public; one fine day the newspapers published the French Communist manifesto in favor of Yugoslavia. Eluard's name, of course, was on it; that day he spoke in Venice. He was booed!

We met every day, sometimes under the arcades of the Piazza della Scala, sometimes in the bar of our hotel, thronged with elegant Italian women with pale silver hair, and we talked. It was fascinating to see Fascism and the war through the eyes of our "Latin brothers." One of them confessed that, born and brought up under the Fascist regime, he had remained loyal to it for a long time. "But the night that Mussolini fell I understood!" he told us, with the accents of a triumphant fanatic. These converts despised the exiles who had been cut off from their homeland by their intransigence and found it difficult to regain a footing in reality; the converts saw their past errors, even their compromises as stages on a journey toward their present political maturity. They kept their virtuous zeal in check by a liberal use of irony. "Now," they told us, "there is a population of ninety million in Italy. Forty-five million who were Fascist; forty-five million who weren't." I remember one of their jokes. An Italian tourist bus was taking some people on a tour of the battlefields; every time they passed through a ruined village a little man, sitting in the back of the bus, started to wring his hands. "It's my fault! It's my fault!" One of the passengers became so curious he asked: "Why is it your fault?" "I'm the only Fascist in the bus." One man, politically a follower of Stendhal, as zealous then as he was now, but under different colors, told us with a laugh that he had been nicknamed "the Black and the Red."

I saw the brick palaces and churches of Milan, but not "The Last Supper," which was undergoing restoration. Vigorelli drove us around Lake Como; he had a little Romanesque chapel at the water's edge opened for us; it was very beautiful, decorated with frescoes by Masolino. He showed us Dongo, the birthplace of Stendhal's Fabrice, and also the place where Mussolini was arrested and his escort butchered. These flowers were watered with blood, he told us, pointing to the bright flower beds reflected in the blue water. In this passionate landscape, we ate ices as smooth as sin, before going on to stay the night at Vigorelli's villa above the lake.

Bompiani, who belonged to the extreme Nationalist Right, told Sartre once more that a left-wing Frenchman was at that particular moment an enemy twice over: he was both an annexer of Brigua and Tenda and a supporter of Tito. If he opened his mouth in public, Sartre would get himself lynched, and what is more he would deserve to be lynched! Our friends were afraid that the neo-Fascists might start a riot. At the entrance to the courtyard where Sartre spoke, and even upon the platform, they stationed policemen armed with sub-machine guns. The courtyard was full; not a boo, nothing but applause. Another evening, I gave a talk in Mme Marzoli's bookstore without causing the slightest disturbance. All this was very compromising for Bompiani, who had wanted to dissociate himself from us entirely. Reluctantly, he invited us to dinner. He lived in a palace; on the ground floor we stepped into an elevator that brought us directly into a salon upstairs; at table, we were waited on by footmen wearing livery and white silk gloves. Bompiani didn't so much as open his mouth; when coffee was served, he seized a newspaper and buried his face in it. The next day he let it be understood that he wasn't going to provide Sartre with the money he had promised, and which we were counting on to allow us to continue our trip.

Luckily, the publisher Arnaldo Mondadori heard of our difficulties through Vittorini, and his son, Alberto, a magnificent moustachioed pirate with a deep bass voice, came and negotiated with Sartre; it was agreed that henceforth Mondadori would be his sole publisher in Italy, and that on the strength of this agreement Sartre was to receive a substantial advance. Alberto also offered to drive us to Venice and then to Florence. We accepted gladly; we both liked him, and we also liked his wife, Virginia, who was exquisitely beautiful and endowed with that naturalness Stendhal prized so much in Italian women. Her lively young sister came with them, and also an architect friend. As we rode along, they laughed and chatted and hummed; at one point they broke off in confusion when they realized that they had all been singing *Giovinezza* at the tops of their voices. I was astounded, in Venice, to find myself living in the Grand Hôtel, in which, in the old days, I never dreamed of setting foot. Restaurants, bars, they knew all the good places; and they also loved Italy, and showed us everything there was to be seen with the gayest erudition. Among so many shining moments, I recall our departure for Florence; dawn was turning into morning as I loaded my baggage into the gondola; I could feel the cool breath of the water and the gentle warmth of the rising sun on my skin. That evening in Florence we prowled for a long time in front of the Signoria; the moonlight reached in under the loggia to caress Cellini's statue, and the architect, too, touched it with emotion. Despite all the deaths, the ruins, the tide of disaster, the beauty was still there.

Mondadori and his wife went back to Venice. We hired a car to go on to Rome; we were lucky enough to run out of gas at the gates of the city or I might never have known the odor of dusk in the Roman Campagna. We had booked rooms at the Plaza Hotel on the Corso, where all the French officials stayed; I missed the Albergo del Sol.

Sartre gave two lectures; and since, at that time, every French writer was a representative of our national prestige, we were shown every consideration. The French cultural attaché took us by car to see the lake and the castle of Bracciano. Jacques Ibert invited us one evening to the Villa Medici; the park was full of bonfires that scented the night air. The French *chargé d'affaires* gave a dinner for us at the Palazzo Farnese; for the first time in my life I wore an evening dress, not *décolletée* but long and black, that the cultural attaché's wife had lent me. I was nervous about these ceremonial occasions, but their formality was softened by the Italians' natural grace. Carlo Levi appeared without a tie, his unbuttoned collar wide open. A few weeks earlier, Jacques Ibert's son had come into the offices of *Les Temps Modernes* with a book in his hand. "It's just been published in Italy and it's having an enormous success; I'm translating it," he told me; it was *Christ Stopped at Eboli*. I read it and we were to publish some long excerpts in November; in it Levi described the life of a village in the South of Italy where he had been forced to live before the war on account of his anti-Fascist beliefs; I had been very taken with the person I could sense behind this account; when he appeared in flesh and blood, I was not disappointed. Doctor, painter, writer, journalist, he belonged to the Action Party, which was the offspring of the "Justice and Liberty" movement started in France by the Rosselli brothers, who had united the democratic bourgeoisie against Fascism; the Action Party, born in Milan in 1941–42, had made a resistance pact with the Italian Socialist and Communist parties; under Parri, it had led the first Resistance government; it was a small group composed mainly of intellectuals and without contact with the masses; a split had occurred a few months earlier between the Liberals within the party and the Revolutionaries, of whom Levi was one, and whose position was very near that of the Communists.[1] Our position was therefore very similar to his. He talked as charmingly as he wrote. He noticed everything, was amused by everything, and his insatiable curiosity reminded me of Giacometti; even death seemed to him an interesting experiment; he described people or things without ever using general ideas but, in the Italian manner, by the use of brief and well-chosen anecdotes. He lived in an enormous studio on the top floor of a palace; at the foot of the monumental staircase—which the noble owner once used to ascend on horseback— there was a marble finger the size of a man; on the wall beside Carlo Levi's door, we read terrible insults scribbled there by the owner who was vainly trying to get him out, and also Levi's replies. We understood why he had dug his heels in: from his windows giving onto the Piazza Gesù, he looked out over the whole of Rome. Amid the motley accumulation of papers, books and canvases cluttering his apartment, he was carefully preserving some dried-up roses. "Anywhere else, they would have fallen to bits long ago," he said. "My presence is beneficent." And he believed his influence was quite as decisive on men as it was on flowers. "I won't have a show this year," he said. "I'm going through a period of research. All the young painters would start imitating me, when I'm not sure what I'm doing myself." Although so convinced of his own importance, he was not the least bit vain about it. He attributed it less to his own merits than to an aura, bestowed upon him in the cradle by some lucky chance and always surrounding him; this atmosphere was a protection against all misfortunes. His optimism amounted practically to a superstition. During the war, he had decided it was pointless to hide and was convinced that a pair of glasses and a moustache were camouflage enough; he was recognizable a hundred yards away; fortunately anti-Semitism never gained a strong hold in Italy. He appreciated all the pleasures of life and displayed toward women an

[1] The Action Party split in 1947. Some of its members enrolled in the Communist Party, some in the Socialist Party; others, like Levi, although their sympathies were with the Communists, remained independent.

affectionate devotion rarely found in Italians; furthermore he was of a romantic disposition; as we left him one evening, we watched with surprise as he climbed up a street lamp and climbed in through a window.

Less expansive in manner, more reticent, Silone—whose *Fontamara* I had liked so much in the old days, and more recently *Bread and Wine*—was also a raconteur; I took great pleasure in his stories about his childhood in the Abruzzi and the hard peasants of the village where he was born.

From 1924 to 1930, he had been one of the main figures and then the leader of the Italian Communist Party, which was in exile at the time; he was expelled from it in 1931, for reasons of which we were ignorant.[1] Back in Italy after the war, he joined the Italian Socialist Party. He talked very little about politics. We were merely struck by his skepticism, which at that time we attributed to his situation as an Italian, rather than to his personal position. At the top of the Janiculum, looking at Rome spread out before us, he said pensively: "How can you expect us to take anything completely seriously! So many centuries superimposed, each one contradicting the rest! Rome has died so many times, and been reborn so many times! It's impossible for an Italian to believe in absolute truth."[2] With great charm, he described what went on behind the scenes in Vatican politics; he told us about the ambivalent attitude of the Italian people—religious, superstitious, but forced into savage anticlericalism by the insistent presence of the clergy. I felt a great sympathy with his wife, an Irishwoman whose pious childhood had been even more stifling than my own.

Moravia we saw very little of. I sat next to him once at a literary luncheon. We got the impression that the Italian writers didn't get on very well among themselves. Sartre's neighbor whispered in his ear: "I'm going to ask you out loud who, in your opinion, is our greatest living novelist, and you answer: Vittorini. Then just watch Moravia's face!" Sartre refused. Whenever an absent colleague's name came up, he was disposed of in two sentences: "Oh! he's not a writer; he's a journalist!" And: "His tragedy is that he didn't know

[1] In 1950, there was a long public controversy on the subject between him and Togliatti. It was published in *Les Temps Modernes*. The least one can say is that from 1927 to 1930 Silone, by his own admission, had played a strange double game.
[2] This relativism, so dear to right-wingers, was doubtless a way of justifying himself. When the Italian Socialist Party split up shortly after, Silone followed Saragat. Soon after, he had become a wholehearted anti-Communist.

how to grow up." Then someone would add: "He still has the mentality of a child"; or: "He's an eternal adolescent." It was as though each of them were throwing back at the others the image of himself he caught in their eyes. We didn't find this malice unpleasant, it seemed to be merely the underside of the acute interest that Italians always have in each other—an improvement, we thought, on our own tepidity.

At the Plaza, we met Scipion who was on his way back from Greece; dining with us one evening in a tavern on Monte Mario, Rome illuminated at our feet, he told us about his fistfight with a monk on Mount Athos who had made an attempt on his virtue; he lamented the Italians' Francophobia: in the course of their embraces, a whore had taken a very dangerous hold on him and cried: "What about Brigua, what about Tenda!" He cut a very grave figure at the Farnese dinner, in a dress suit lent him by the cultural attaché.

Jeanine Bouissounouse and her husband Louis de Villefosse, the French representative at the Allied Commission, took us in their car to Frascati and Nemi; they introduced us to their Italian friends: Donnini, a Communist and professor of religious history, who had been in exile for a long while; Bandinelli, the Director General of Fine Arts, also a Communist, who had started a peasant cooperative on his property in Tuscany; Guttuso, a Communist painter who invited us to spend an evening in his studio on the Via Margutta. With its layers of terraces, hidden courtyards, staircases and catwalks, this street, inhabited mainly by painters and writers, had become a veritable *maquis* during the Roman Resistance. I visited the Ardeatini quarries, next to the Catacombs. As a reprisal for an attack that had cost the lives of thirty-three Germans, three hundred and thirty Resistance members were machine-gunned here on March 24, 1944. The Germans abandoned the bodies in the quarry and then blocked the entrance by dynamiting the sides; the corpses were not found until three months later. In 1946, the memory of these victims (cooled, a few years later, by marble) was still fresh; the wooden coffins lay in rows along the galleries, flat on the tawny ground, each one marked with a name and two dates; the only ornaments were a few wilting flowers and photos of each victim at his first Communion, at his wedding, as a soldier, in soccer clothes.

The returned exiles with whom we talked in Rome held the recent converts to anti-Fascism in pretty low esteem; we were struck by this conflict between the intransigents—mostly quite old men—

and the realists of the rising generation; these latter seemed to us much better adapted to the new situation than the exiles.[1]

We spent two days in Naples. The city had suffered a great deal. The only hotel which was open was falling to pieces; you could see the sky through gaping holes in the ceilings; the staircase was covered with rubble; the harbor and the district surrounding it was one intricate ruin. In the hot streets, the wind raised sandstorms from the dust of the disaster. The museum was closed. On Capri, which had been untouched, I rediscovered my past. We stayed a few more days in Rome, at the Hotel della Città, without meeting anyone.

We were very happy to see Italy again, but even happier to find there the atmosphere we had known, for such a short while, after the Liberation. In France, that unity had been achieved, in opposition to a foreign occupation, on the equivocal basis of nationalism; the Left and the Right were bound to move apart again, once the circumstances that forced them together had disappeared. In Italy, the Nationalists were the Fascists; the coalition which opposed them was unanimous in its desire for freedom and democracy; its coherence was a product of its principles and not of events; for this reason it survived the war; Liberals, Socialists and Communists united against the Right to make sure the new constitution was respected. The sincerity of the republican and democratic positions of the Italian Communist Party was never at any time doubted by its allies. The German-Soviet pact and the uncertainty it caused among the French Communists provided a weapon against them; the record of the Italian Communists' resistance to Fascism remained without a blot; all the anti-Fascists—which is to say, at that time, almost the whole country—paid tribute to their courage.

The situation of the Italian Communist Party was more favorable than that of the French for reasons that dated back many years. In France, the bourgeoisie, having made a success of its Revolution in 1789, went on without hesitation to wage an all-out war against the working class. In Italy, the bourgeoisie rose to the position of a ruling class only in the nineteenth century, after many divisions and crises; in the course of this upward movement it was forced, especially at the beginning of the twentieth century, to accept the support of the proletariat. This collusion had important cultural conse-

---

1 There were also men in Italy who were intransigent and realistic at the same time; the anti-Fascists who had fought on the spot, in secret. But we only met these later.

quences. A bourgeois philosopher like Labriola, initially a Hegelian, found the approach to Marxism easy. This widening of bourgeois thought produced a reciprocal effect in the thought of the Marxists. In one brilliant synthesis, Gramsci, a Marxist, was able to use the whole of bourgeois humanist thought for his own purposes. History presented the Italian Communists with still more good luck. After the First World War, the ebb of the European proletariat sent Italy into Fascism and the Italian Communists into hiding; they fought within their own country, which meant they were spared many risks. The French Communist Party, a minority with scarcely any influence in their own country, took internationalism as its primary objective; obedient to the directives of the Comintern, obliged to endorse Stalin's politics *in toto*—including, among other things, the Moscow trials—it came to be viewed as "the Foreigners' Party," and this unpopularity was the cause of its subsequent rigidity. During the Resistance it earned letters patent for patriotism, and in the elections won more votes than either of the other two parties; still it did not become a party of the masses. France in 1945 had an industrial and stratified society; the interests of the peasants were not the same as those of the workers; and even among the latter there were different layers in conflict. The Communists were recruited mainly from among the salaried workers. Despite the large number of votes they won, the number of Party members continued to be low; to remain strong they needed to make themselves into a bloc without a flaw.

Italy, lacking iron and coal—almost an underdeveloped country—was still in a state of flux; there was no great distance between the workers and the peasants, many of whom—especially in the South—constituted a revolutionary force. Above all, both peasants and workers, deeply marked by the memory of Fascism whose corpse was then still warm, believed that Communism alone was capable of consolidating its defeat. The Italian Communist Party therefore had solid foundations in the population as a whole. Not finding itself cut off or enclosed on any level, it had no tendency to interpret differences of opinion as constituting opposition. In particular it considered the Italian intellectuals, who were all leftist and all sympathizers, as friends and not as adversaries.

Its alliance with the Italian Socialists also contributed to its freedom from the isolation which so beset the French Communists. As a result of the rupture brought about by the Fascists, the Italian Socialist Party under Nenni had been able to renew itself; and it had decided, after so many years of united struggle, to maintain its friendly relations with the Communists. In France, the Socialists had inherited everything from the S.F.I.O., including its anti-Communism. If the French Communist Party regarded all non-Communists as enemies, it was for the good reason that in most cases that is what they were; mistrust, justified by the situation, forbade them to make exceptions.

At the time we did not clearly understand the differences we observed between the Communists in the two countries; but, saddened by the hostility at home, we profited from the friendship of the Italians with a pleasure which, over a period of sixteen years, has never been belied.

I left Sartre in Milan to spend three weeks exploring the Dolomites. My first night alone was spent at Merano; it remains one of my most precious memories. I ate dinner and drank white wine in a courtyard hung with ivy, opposite a copper-faced clock that seemed to watch over me from high up on the wall; it had been a long time since I had contemplated several weeks of mountains and silence stretching ahead of me: unhappiness and dangers that I now knew about added to my joy a dimension of pathos that made my eyes mist over.

Bolzano, its hillsides covered with pale vines, Vitipino, its streets gay as a travelogue—I explored all the Austrian part of Italy. And also, from peak to peak, from one mountain hut to the next, across alps and rocks, I walked. Once more I smelled the grass, heard the noise of pebbles rolling down the screes, experienced again the gasping effort of the long climb, the ecstasy of relief when the haversack slips from the shoulders that lean back against the earth, the early departures under the pale sky, the pleasure of following the curve of the day from dawn to dusk.

One evening, in the heart of the mountains, a long way from any road, in a mountain inn, I asked for a room and dinner; they served me, but without a word, without a smile. On the wall I noticed the photograph of a young man hung with a piece of black crepe. As I rose from the table, the woman who ran the place managed to get out one word: "Tedesca?" No! I said, I was French. Their faces lighted up. My Italian, they explained, had a German terseness about it. And the son of the house had been killed in the *maquis*.

It was one of my hardest journeys on foot, one of the most beautiful and—as I knew then in my heart—the last.

When I got back to Paris, I learned the details of the "Existentialist crime" which had kept the newspapers in copy for weeks. B.[1] owned a little house at Gif-sur-Yvette which he used to lend to Francis Vintenon during the week and then go and spend the weekend there himself. One Saturday morning, as he told it to us, he couldn't find the key in the usual hiding place; the door wasn't locked. Francis is still asleep, he thought, and hoping to surprise him with his girl friend, he tiptoed along the hall; there was a very funny smell in the house. "I went into the bedroom," he said, "gave one look at the bed and exclaimed: 'A Negro!' " It was Francis, his face blackened, a bullet in his temple, his body half burned up by phosphorus. Someone had seen a man with a beard prowling around the village; B. and his friend the painter Patrix both wore beards; they were questioned; they had had nothing to do with the murder. It seems that Vintenon, who had entered the Resistance movement in 1943, was killed by an ex-collaborator; a name was even mentioned, but the matter was hushed up.

An Italian director wanted to make a film of *No Exit*. Sartre returned to Rome at the end of September to work on the scenario and discuss it with him; I accompanied him; Lefèvre-Pontalis, whom he had asked to help him, came along with his wife. We set up headquarters at our old favorite, the Minerva Hotel, right in the center of town. I had never seen Rome in the gentle October light, and I had never been free enough from social obligations and sightseeing to spend quiet days simply working. But now, when I was living there as though the city's beauty were a mere accessory, a delightful familiarity grew up between us; there were still many unexpected ways for me to explore the good things of this world.

Thanks to Soupault, who had got me invitations from a great many American universities, it was definitely decided that I was going to America; the office of the Relations Culturelles had agreed to pay my plane fare over; I was due to go in January. The whole three months beforehand were illuminated by this fact. For me it was a period of feverish activity. The past two years had not stifled my

[1] One of Sartre's ex-pupils, who had become a doctor.

happiness; now it was difficult to know what to feed it with. I could not give up the old illusions, yet I had ceased to believe in them. Political decisions were becoming increasingly difficult, and our friendships were being affected by our hesitations in this area.

Despite the imperious counsels of De Gaulle, who had re-entered public life with his knightly, copybook speeches, the French people had accepted the Constitution proposed by the National Assembly. In the November elections, the Communists resumed their position as the leading political party in France. But the M.R.P. remained powerful. The Gaullist Union was growing stronger; we had no thought of moving away from the Communists, despite their continuing enmity (a novel by Kanapa about the Resistance was published in which Sartre was depicted as a conceited blockhead, a coward and almost an agent provocateur). In reply to Koestler's *Arrival and Departure* and his more recent book *The Yogi and the Commissar,* Merleau-Ponty wrote a piece in *Les Temps Modernes* called "The Yogi and the Proletarian." In it he clarified the meaning of the Moscow trials, especially Bukharin's. The reality of our acts escapes us, he wrote, but it is on that reality that we are judged and not on our intentions; although he is unable to predict exactly what that reality will be, man as politician must assume it at the moment he makes any decision, and he never has the right to wash his hands of it afterwards. In 1936, in a Soviet Russia isolated, threatened, and unable to preserve the Revolution except at the price of a monolithic severity, all opposition assumed the objective aspect of treason. Merleau-Ponty reminded the Russians that, inversely, the traitors were merely those in the opposition. He subordinated morality to history much more resolutely than any Existentialist had ever done. We crossed this Rubicon with him, conscious that moralism—although we were not yet free of it ourselves—was the last bastion of bourgeois idealism. His essay diverged too far from orthodox Marxism to be well received by the Communists. The Right waxed indignant; he was accused of writing an apology for Stalinism.

Camus found our position distasteful. His anti-Communism had already caused dissension between us; in November of '45, as he was driving me home, he had defended De Gaulle against Thorez; as I was leaving him he shouted through the car window: "At least General de Gaulle cuts a better figure than M. Jacques Duclos!" Such an ill-tempered way of arguing surprised me, coming from him. At present his position was a long way from De Gaulle's, but even fur-

ther from the Communists. He came back from New York with even
less sympathy for the U.S.A. than Sartre had had, but this didn't
decrease his hostility toward the U.S.S.R. in the slightest. While he
was away, Aron and Ollivier had used *Combat* to support the
S.F.I.O. which now drew most of its members from the lower middle
classes; Camus did not dissociate himself from them. Shortly after his
return, Bost was going to see him in his office and passed Aron on the
way out as he was saying in a sarcastic tone: "Well, I must be off to
write my reactionary editorial." Camus expressed astonishment; Bost
made it clear to him what he thought about the paper's current policy. "If you don't like it, why don't you leave?" Camus asked. "I'm
going to," said Bost. He broke with *Combat* and Camus was indignant: "There's gratitude!" However, if Camus stopped writing in
Combat for a long while, it was because he resented, or so I was told,
Aron's increasing influence there. But I think he was also disillu-
sioned with politics in general, which he had entered only because he
envisaged it as "a direct address of man to other men," in other
words, from the moral point of view. Sartre took him up on this
confusion of ideas one day: "*Combat* is too concerned with moral
issues at the expense of political ones." Camus denied the accusation.
Yet the article with which he made his reappearance in the newspaper in November 1946, entitled "Neither Victims nor Exe-
cutioners," was still really concerned with ethical considerations.
He had no taste for the deliberations and the risks entailed in
political thought; he had to be sure of his ideas so that he could be
sure of himself. His reaction to the contradictions of the political
situation was to detach himself from it, and Sartre's efforts to adjust
to them made him impatient. Existentialism irritated him. When he
read the first part of my *Ethics of Ambiguity* in *Les Temps Modernes*, he offered a few acid observations; in his eyes, I was sinning
against *la clarté française;* we, on our side, found that he sometimes
failed to pursue his thought as far as he might, simply in order to live
up to this ideal; not through any irresponsibility, but because these
were his principles; he was protecting himself. It is hard to depend
on others when one has believed oneself to be a sovereign individual.
This illusion is common to all bourgeois intellectuals, and we were
none of us cured of it too easily. In all of us, our ethical thinking was
an attempt to regain that pre-eminence. But Sartre, and myself in his
wake, had thrown a great deal of our ballast overboard; yesterday's
values had been stripped from us by the existence of the masses—

magnanimity, to which we had clung so savagely, and even authenticity. As he searched, Sartre sometimes groped blindly, but always remained open. Camus was keeping himself covered. He had an idea of himself which no task, no revelation, would have made him give up. Our relations remained very cordial; but from time to time a shadow darkened them; these fluctuations were due much more to Camus than to Sartre and myself. He admitted that when he was with us he couldn't help sympathizing with us, but that when he was away from us we angered him.

In October, a tumultuous newcomer burst into our group: Koestler, whose play *Twilight Bar* was about to be put on in Paris. Friends of his had assured us that his anti-Stalinism had not forced him over to the Right; he had told an American newspaper that if he had been a Frenchman he would rather live in exile in Patagonia than under De Gaulle's dictatorship.

We met first at the Pont-Royal. He accosted Sartre with pleasing simplicity: "Hello. I'm Koestler." We saw him next in the apartment where Sartre had just gone to live with his mother in the Place Saint-Germain-des-Prés. In a peremptory tone, softened by an almost feminine smile, he told Sartre: "You are a better novelist than I am, but not such a good philosopher." He was in the process of writing a summa of philosophy whose main outlines he described to us: he wanted to assure man a margin of freedom without departing from physiological materialism. Taking his inspiration from works which we both knew, he explained to us that the systems governed by the cerebellum, the thalamus and the lower brain overlapped but did not rigidly control each other; between the lower and the upper parts there must be room for a "bubble" of liberty. It reminded me of *La Contingence des Lois de la Nature* by Boutroux, and I thought to myself that Koestler was certainly a better novelist than he was a philosopher; he made me want to laugh when he talked about the thalamus, because he pronounced it thalamoose, and I couldn't help thinking of the cakes I used to eat as a child, called *talmousses*. That day we were a bit embarrassed by his self-taught pedantry, by the doctrinaire self-assurance and the scientism he had retained from his rather mediocre Marxist training. This embarrassment persisted. With Camus we never talked about each other's books, whereas Koestler was continually exclaiming every other minute: "You must read what I wrote about that!" Success had gone to his head; he was vain and full of self-importance. But he was also full of warmth, life and curiosity; the passion with which he argued was unflagging; he was always ready, at any hour of the day or night, to talk about any subject under the sun. He was generous with his time, with himself, and also with his money; he had no taste for ostentation, but when one went out with him he always wanted to pay for everything and never counted the cost. He had a naïve pride in the fact that his wife, Mamaine, belonged to an aristocratic English family. She was very blond, very pretty, with a sharp wit; graceful and fragile, she was already suffering from the lung infection to which she succumbed some ten years later.

During the three or four weeks he spent in Paris, we met Koestler often, usually with Camus; they were very close. Bost went with us once and the conversation degenerated into an argument because Bost defended the politics of the Communist Party. "You shouldn't have brought him, it was wrong of you," Koestler told us severely the next day; he disliked young people; he felt excluded from their future, and any exclusion seemed to him a condemnation. Touchy, tormented, greedy for human warmth, but cut off from others by his personal obsessions—"I have my Furies," he used to say—Koestler's relations with us were always fluctuating. One evening we had dinner with him, Mamaine, Camus, Francine, and then went on to a little dance hall in the Rue des Gravilliers; then he issued an imperious invitation to the Shéhérézade; normally neither Camus nor myself would ever have set foot in that sort of place. Koestler ordered *zakouski*, vodka, champagne. The following afternoon, Sartre was to give a lecture at the Sorbonne, under the aegis of Unesco, on "The Writer's Responsibility," and he hadn't yet prepared it. But the alcohol, the gypsy music and above all the heat of our discussions made him lose track of the time. Camus returned to a theme very dear to him: "If only it were possible to tell the truth!" Koestler grew gloomy as he listened to "Dark Eyes." "It's impossible to be friends if you differ about politics!" he said in an accusing tone. He rehashed his old grudges against Stalin's Russia, accusing Sartre and even Camus of trying to compromise with the Soviets. We didn't take his lugubriousness seriously; we were not aware of the passionate depths of his anti-Communism. While Koestler continued his monologue, Camus said to us: "What we have in common, you and I, is that for us individuals come first; we prefer the concrete to the abstract, people to doctrines, we place friendship above politics." We agreed, with an exaltation partly caused by alcohol and the lateness of the hour. Koestler repeated: "Impossible! Impossible!" And I replied, in a low voice, but clearly: "It *is* possible; and we are the proof of it at this very moment, since, despite all our dissensions, we are so happy to be together." Politics had opened abysses between some people and ourselves; but we still thought that nothing separated us from Camus except a few nuances of terminology.

At four in the morning, we went to have something to eat and some more to drink at a bistro in Les Halles. Koestler was very jumpy; whether in irritation or in fun, he threw a crust of bread across the table and hit Mamaine right in the eye; he apologized and sobered up a bit; Sartre kept giggling: "To think that in a few hours I'm going to give a talk on the writer's responsibility!" and Camus laughed. I was laughing too, but alcohol has always made me much more inclined to weep, and when I found myself alone with Sartre in the streets of Paris at dawn I began to sob over the tragedy of the human condition; as we crossed the Seine, I leaned on the parapet of the bridge. "I don't see why we don't throw ourselves into the river!" "All right, then, let's throw ourselves in!" said Sartre, who was finding my tears contagious and had shed a few himself. We got home at about eight in the morning. When I saw Sartre again at four in the afternoon his face was ravaged; he had slept for two or three hours and then stuffed himself full of orthedrine in order to get his lecture prepared. I thought to myself as I went into the packed amphitheater: "If they had seen Sartre at six this morning!"

Through Koestler, we met Manès Sperber, whom Koestler considered his master and the most competent psychologist of our age. He had a reticent charm; but he was a rigid Adlerian, a fanatical anti-Communist, and we found his dogmatism repellent. He told us that Malraux had been talking to him about a Russian secret weapon even more terrible than the atomic bomb: suitcases, quite innocent in appearance, containing radioactive dust; members of the fifth column—that is, Communists—would place these on a given day in previously selected spots, and then, after setting a certain mechanism in motion, they would steal away; the inhabitants of Chicago, New York, Pittsburgh, Detroit would die like flies. It was understandable that, faced with such a danger, the Right should advocate a War of Prevention.

About two weeks after our evening with Koestler, Boris Vian and his wife gave a party; there were a great many people there, including Merleau-Ponty. Vian had published several *Chroniques du Men-*

teur in *Les Temps Modernes,* as well a a short story, *Les Fourmis,* and some extracts from *L'Écume des Jours,* whose failure he had apparently taken in good humor. That evening, while listening to jazz, we talked a lot about Vernon Sullivan, the author of the novel *I Spit on Your Grave,* which Vian had just translated: there was a rumor going around that Sullivan didn't exist. At about eleven, Camus arrived in a bad temper, having just got back from a trip to the Midi; he attacked Merleau-Ponty on the subject of his article, "The Yogi and the Proletarian," accused him of justifying the Moscow trials and was appalled that opposition could be made into treason. Merleau-Ponty defended himself, Sartre supported him; Camus shattered, left, slamming the door behind him; Sartre and Bost rushed out and ran after him along the street, but he refused to come back. This quarrel was to last until March 1947.

Why such an outburst? I think that Camus was going through a crisis caused by the feeling that his golden age was drawing to a close. He had known several years of triumph; he was attractive, people liked him. "People thought I had charm, think of it! Do you know what charm is? It's a way of hearing oneself say yes, without having asked any definite question."[1] His good luck went to his head; he thought there were no limits to what he could do: "As success succeeded success, I began to think of myself, though I hesitate to admit it, as *chosen.*" The success of *The Stranger* and the triumph of the Resistance had convinced him that everything he undertook must be crowned with victory. We were with him once at a concert which everyone who was anyone in Paris attended; he was accompanied by a young singer in whom he was interested. "When I think," he said to Sartre, "that we can foist her on this public tomorrow!" He swept the auditorium with a triumphant gesture. Sartre, at his request, wrote the first words of a song: "Hell is all my habit now." But that was as far as it went. During lunch with me one day at the Petit Saint-Benoît, shortly after Hiroshima, he told me that in order to prevent an atomic war, he was going to ask all the great scientists in the world to stop their researches. "Isn't that a bit Utopian?" I objected. He flared up immediately. "They also said it was Utopian to want to liberate Paris ourselves. To be realistic means to dare." I was used to these haughty fits of temper; afterward, without openly admitting it, he would compromise. He never mentioned this project to me again. He saw quickly enough that nothing was ever as easy as he had

[1] *The Fall.*

supposed; instead of facing them squarely, he would back down when confronted with obstacles. One day when I was preparing a lecture, he gave me a piece of advice that left me flabbergasted: "If someone asks you an embarrassing question, answer it with another question." Students were more than once disappointed by his evasions. He skipped through books instead of reading them; he made up his mind beforehand instead of thinking things out. I mentioned earlier that discretion masked this laziness. He loved the nature he ruled over, but history was a threat to his individuality and he refused to bow before it. It was this very refusal that laid him open to attack; it made him, instead of "an exemplary reality," into "the empty affirmation of an ideal," as Sartre wrote in 1952. He fought against this intrusion rather than summon the strength to rid himself of his old dreams. Little by little, rancor began to collect in his heart, against the resistance of his opponents, against systems of philosophy, against the world in general. They seemed to him injustices and therefore wounded him, for he believed in his rights over things and people; he was generous and expected acknowledgment of it; the word that came immediately to his lips when he was contradicted or criticized was ingratitude. Until, later on, he reached the point, overwhelmed though he had once been with success, of hoping "to die without hatred."[1]

In November, *The Victors* opened. Sartre had written this play a year before; at the time when the ex-collaborators were beginning to show themselves again, he had wanted to refresh people's memories. He had thought a great deal about torture for four whole years; alone, and among friends, he asked himself: Should I not speak about it too? What would be the best way to handle it? He had also pondered a great deal on the relation between the torturer and his victim. All these thoughts that haunted him he threw into his play. Once more he confronted ethics and *praxis:* Lucie retreats stubbornly into her individualistic pride, while the militant Communist, presented by Sartre as in the right, aims at effectiveness.

Sartre had given the parts to Vitold, Cuny, Vibert, Chauffard and Marie Olivier. Vitold was to direct. But it hadn't been easy finding a producer and a theater. While Sartre was away in America, I spent countless hours of exasperation looking. The torture scene scared people off. "Given my position during the war," said Hébertot, "I just can't allow myself to put on a play of this sort." After letting me

[1] *La Mer au Plus Près.*

hope that he would do it at the Théâtre de L'Oeuvre, Beer slunk away too. Finally Simone Berriau, who had just taken on the Théâtre Antoine again, accepted it. Masson did the scenery. To make up a full bill, Sartre spent a few days writing *The Respectful Prostitute*, inspired by a true story that he had read in Pozner's *États Désunis*. The tortures in *The Victors* took place almost entirely behind the scenery; seen from the wings they weren't very frightening, and even made us laugh, since the martyr, Vitold, always famished at that hour, would hurl himself on a sandwich as soon as he got off stage and bolt it between shrieks. On opening night I was in the audience, and everything changed. I had experienced before the process by which a game without consequence is transformed into an event; but this time, as the cautious theater managers had predicted, the fruit of this metamorphosis was a scandal. It even affected me; hearing them with the ears of the other spectators, Vitold's shrieks were almost intolerable. Mme Stève Passeur stood up and shouted, very straight underneath her hat: "It's a disgrace!" In the orchestra, people even came to blows. Aron's wife left at intermission, having almost fainted, and he followed her. The meaning of this uproar was clear: the bourgeoisie was initiating a reunification, and to awaken such unpleasant memories seemed the height of bad taste. Sartre himself was strongly affected by the anxiety he was causing; the first few nights, when it came time for the torture scene, he would drink whisky to ward it off, and often zigzagged a bit on his way home. The bourgeois critics talked about Grand Guignol, and censured Sartre for reviving old hatreds. A new gutter-press weekly, *Franc-Dimanche*, sent a reporter to his home who took a photograph as soon as the door was opened and published it as a picture of Sartre's mother: it was someone else. They also published an article even more nauseating than the one in *Samedi-Soir* a year earlier.

Almost simultaneously, at the Marigny, Barrault put on Salacrou's *Les Nuits de la Colère*, which was also about the Resistance. Technically he had borrowed a great deal from the cinema, and used flashbacks and fades; we were very impressed by the conversations in which Madeleine Renaud and Jean Desailly gradually shifted from neutrality to treason; the "positive" side of the play came over less well. In the same way, the conversations of the soldiers in *The Victors* came off better than those of their victims. Portraits of heroism are not profitable; for two such clever dramatists as Sartre and Salacrou to have risked the attempt, the ethical trend of that period must have been almost irresistible.[1] A little later, in January of 1947, Mouloudji's play *Quatre femmes* was acted at the Théâtre de la Renaissance; it had been inspired by Lola's detention in prison camp and depicted the daily life of four women prisoners. The play was not successful; the critics repeated irritably that it was time to bury the past.

The Communists, generally speaking, had supported *The Victors*. Yet when Sartre saw Ehrenburg for the first time, at a lunch organized by Sartre's theatrical agent, the publisher Nagel, Ehrenburg reproached him bitterly for having depicted the members of the Resistance as cowards and traitors. Sartre couldn't believe his ears. "Have you read the play?" Ehrenburg admitted that he had merely skimmed through the first scene or two, but his mind was made up. "If I got that impression, there must have been some reason for it." As for *The Respectful Prostitute,* the Communists thought it a pity Sartre had shown his public a Negro trembling with fear and respect, instead of a real fighter. "That's because my play reflects the present impossibility of solving the color problem in the U.S."[2] Sartre replied. But the Communists' conception of what literature should be was very rigidly fixed, and one of their grievances was that he wouldn't comply with it.

What they wanted to see were great, inspiring works: something epic, something optimistic. Sartre did too, but in his own way. He has explained himself on the subject in his unpublished notes. He refused to accept hope as an assumption, "hope *a priori.*" At that time he saw action as an intermediary idea between a certain ethical system inspired by the Resistance and the realism of *praxis;* the undertaking is not to be based on a calculation of chances; it is itself the only hope permitted. The writer should not sing of some glorious possible future but depict the world as it is, and thereby arouse the will to change it. The more convincing the picture he presents, the better he will attain this end; even the darkest of works is not pessimistic, once one accepts that it is a rallying cry for freedom, that it exists only as a function of freedom. Thus, *The Respectful Prostitute* provokes the indignation of the spectators, while, on the other hand,

---

[1] Public gossip, and Henri Jeanson especially, attributed to Sartre the malicious comment that "Salacrou does better with his collaborators than with his Resistance members, because he knows them better." What Sartre said was that Salacrou knew the middle classes better, in general, than the *dinamiteros* of the Resistance.

[2] This was in 1946.

Lizzie's efforts to escape from her hoaxed condition suggest the possibility that she may succeed. Moreover, Sartre understood the Communist point of view on this matter: on the level of the masses, hope
is one of the elements of action; the struggle is too hard for them to
risk entering it unless they believe in their ultimate victory. What he
called "a hard optimism" was suitable only for a public that did not
experience reality as a painful daily struggle for life; reflection is
necessary, and perspective, and trust, if one is to transcend the critical attitude instead of becoming bogged down in it. When *The
Respectful Prostitute* was made into a film, he changed the ending of
his own accord: Lizzie perseveres in her attempt to save the innocent
Negro. The style of the play, harsh but comic, kept the original
dénouement at a distance; in the film it would have appeared true
but vile. And then, when one demonstrates to people privileged
enough to go to a theater that there exist today situations that are
both appalling and without remedy, one disturbs them, one shakes
them up. Well and good; but a film is shown to millions of spectators
to whom their own lives are appalling situations without remedy:
any defeat is their defeat too; merely adding to their discouragement
is a betrayal. Sartre noted, several years later: *"The Communists are
right. I am not wrong. For people who are tired and crushed, hope is
always a necessity. They have only too many occasions for despair.
But one must also maintain the possibility of an undertaking embarked upon without illusions."* He did maintain that possibility.[1]

I was working on my essay and keeping busy at *Les Temps Modernes*. Every time I opened a manuscript I had a sense of adventure. I
read English and American books no one had heard of in France.

---

[1] In his plays and novels, Sartre is very close to the esthetic defined with reference
to the novel by the younger Lukács. For Lukács, says Goldmann, in an introduction
to his early writings (*Les Temps Modernes*, August 1962), "the hero of the novel is a
problematic being"; he "is searching for absolute values in an inauthentic and corrupt
mode." The world of a novel "cannot possibly include a positive hero, for the simple
reason that all the values which govern it are *implicit,* and therefore in relation to
those values all the people in the novel have a character that is both positive and
negative at the same time." But as soon as literature is directed to the oppressed and
not to the privileged, simply to pose the problem without at least sketching a solution
is not enough. In 1955 we discovered Lousin, the great Chinese writer of the later
thirties, and were amazed to discover that he had gone through a quarrel with his
Communist comrades analogous to Sartre's own: he offered a description of the society
around him, in which revolution was for the time being impossible, that was purely
critical; he was asked to give some picture of what its future was to be. In the end he
consented, yielding to the imperatives of action; but he was of the opinion that from
this time on, his works no longer possessed the slightest esthetic value. Brecht was long
suspect in the U.S.S.R. for the same reasons: his weapon is irony, not virtuous
sentiments.

Every Tuesday I joined the selection committee at Gallimard. There were moments of gaiety, mostly when Paulhan carefully tore a book to pieces and concluded: "Of course we must publish it." Once a week, we received in the offices of the magazine people who brought us material and suggestions, or who came to ask our advice. A great deal had been written during the past few years that neither the press nor the publishers as yet had the material resources to print; the tide of testimony was rising. I was always happy when I could tell an author that his work had been accepted; though less so when we were forced to cut: every line seemed essential to the man who had written it. An even more ungrateful task was having to say no. The writer would object, he would prove to you that his article was good, that he was talented. He would leave convinced that he was the victim of some conspiracy. There were young ones who were determined to succeed straightaway, at any cost; there were the old ones trying for the last time; misunderstood ones who dreamed of escaping from the humdrum routine of home life; the men and women of every age who needed the money. Many were seeking in all sincerity for a sort of salvation in literature, but most of them wanted to obtain it at a discount, without paying the fair price in work, trouble and care. Generally speaking, they had some very strange ideas about how much you could earn by writing. One young woman entrusted me with the manuscript of a novel in which the heroine was torn between a loathsome middle-class husband and a working-class lover endowed with all the virtues; the heroine wrote down her story, a publisher accepted it, she made a vast amount of money and went off on a cruise with the man she loved. Among other things, I criticized the angelic conception of the lover. "I understand how you feel," she said, "but you don't know him. He really is like that!" Two years later she wrote me: "Your criticism was quite right; I was taken in; he was playing a game with me; he wasn't the man I took him for." Sometimes I laughed; at other times I felt there was something slightly sinister in all these wild and humble ambitions fermenting in our office. Sometimes we came very close to tragedy; often we descended to pure farce. One of our most troublesome visitors was the Abbé Gengenbach, a semi-defrocked surrealist, who insulted his cloth, drank prodigiously, openly carried on liaisons with women, and then periodically shut himself up in a monastery to repent. He used to come and offer us material, often quite sensational, and ask for money; drink tended to make him rather vehement. One day he talked to me about Breton. "But why does he hate God?" he asked, beginning to weep so copiously that I led him into an empty room. One of our secretaries suddenly dashed through the room as though shot from a gun: an author we had rejected had just slashed his wrists in Lemarchand's office.

In November, I went to Holland on a lecture tour. "Two years ago I weighed nearly forty pounds more than I do now," I was informed by the young woman who met me at the station in Amsterdam. Everyone talked about the famine. The parks were stripped bare; all the trees had been chopped down to fill the fireplaces. The old lady who showed me around Rotterdam took me across vast stretches of empty lots: "This used to be the old residental district; my house stood here." The entire town had been reduced to rubble. The country was taking a long time to recover; in the shop-windows, only "ersatz" products were displayed; the big department stores were empty; to buy even the smallest article one had to produce a card. I came back to Paris with my pockets full of florins I hadn't managed to spend.

I knew how the Dutch had resisted the Occupation; I felt friendly toward almost everyone I met there. Nevertheless, the official side of the trip was tedious. To give myself up to the beauty of the towns, to the riches in the museums, I needed solitude; people were so kind to me I was never alone for a second. Once or twice I rebelled openly; more often I tried cunning; I went to Haarlem on a morning train and pretended I wasn't returning till the evening; that way I was able to look at the Franz Hals collection without witnesses.

A week later, Sartre joined me; he had been to the opening of *Twilight Bar:* a disaster. We looked at Rembrandts and Vermeers together: a little patch of red wall as moving as the yellow wall Proust loved so much. "Why is it so beautiful?" Sartre wondered; we were riding in a train through moorlands, and I listened to him with a curiosity that fifteen years of familiarity had not blunted. Those painted red bricks were the starting point of the definition of art which he put forward a few weeks later in *What Is Literature?:* the reassumption of the world by a freedom.

We spent two days in Utrecht; there we observed the ravages caused by Italian influence reflected in the work of the local artists; vigorous and truthful at first, after a journey to Florence they painted nothing but fashionable trifles. We visited the Psychological

Institute run by Van Lennep. He had written to Sartre and conferred with him in Paris; how far does any *projected action* imply an
evasion, he wanted to know, and this question touched me deeply: I
had always been tempted to regard any occupation as a diversion.
Van Lennep put us through a graphology test; he had invented an
apparatus that enabled him to measure the pressure, the speed and
the rhythm of the subject's strokes as he was writing; after that, our
handwriting was projected, many times enlarged, on a screen. The
contrasts between them were so glaring that the technicians present
were quite upset on our account. We also took some visual tests
invented by Van Lennep, and still not widely known. He showed us
pictures of a galloping horse, a motorboat, a train and a man walking: which one gave us the most immediate impression of speed? The
man, I said, without hesitation; his was the only case in which speed
seemed to me consciously experienced. Also without hesitation,
Sartre chose the motorboat, because it *tears itself away* from the
surface it devours. My answer made him laugh, and I laughed at his,
each of us seeing the other's reaction as a naïve self-disclosure.

We returned to Paris. Calder was having a show of his Mobiles
which had never been seen before in France. Sartre had met him in
America and found great charm in these "little local celebrations";
he wrote the preface to the catalogue. Tall, potbellied, his big
chubby face haloed by thick white hair, Calder seemed to have been
created as he was for the express purpose of recalling, amid his airy
creations, the heaviness of matter. One of his pastimes was making
jewelry; the day of the vernissage he gave me a spiral brooch which I
wore for a long while.

We were seeing a great many people and, since 1943, I had not
changed my opinion: in the writers and artists whose work I liked,
there was always something that awakened my sympathy for them
personally. Though I was surprised, all the same, to find that some of
them had defects that limited this response: vanity or self-importance. Instead of living in the reciprocity of one's relation with the
reader, one turns back toward oneself, one apprehends oneself in the
dimension of the Other; that is vanity. In young people I find it
almost touching; it is a sign of their ingenuous confidence in others.
But this freshness soon evaporates; prolonged, naïveté becomes mere
childishness, and confidence servility. Someone who is blissfully vain
may be very pleasant company, even though he talks too much about
himself, but he is an object of ridicule; he is a dupe; he will take any

courtesy at face value. Thwarted, he will retreat into fantasy and provide for himself what he cannot win from others; or he will become bitter, and the aroma of his simmering rancors and revenges will not be pleasant. He cheats, in any case; his complacency is belied by the dependency he submits to; begging for flattery, he abases himself by the very means he uses to boost his self-esteem. Gazing too long and too lovingly at his own image of himself, he ends up its prisoner; he inevitably falls into the self-importance which is the vehemence of vanity.

Each time I recognize it in a colleague, I am aghast. How can anyone destroy himself for the sake a mask? But I have learned that it is foolish to discount the reality of this problem; the image we present to others is one we must assume; further, if one has abilities it is good to employ them, it is legitimate, if the need arises, to avail oneself of them; a man's truth includes his objective existence and his past, but it is not inevitably limited to such fossilizations. It is in their name that the self-important man denies the perpetual newness of life and becomes in his own eyes the Authority against which all judgment shipwrecks; to the ever-renewed questions that are put to him, instead of trying to think out answers honestly, he looks them up in Holy Writ—in his Work; or else he cites himself as an example, as he once was; by such repetitions, whatever the original brilliance of his successes, he drops behind the rest of the world, and ends up a museum piece. This sclerosis always involves hypocrisy: if one really does think one's opinions at all worthwhile, why shelter behind one's name, one's reputation, one's past achievements? The self-important man either affects contempt for people or demands their respect. This is because he hasn't the courage to face them as equals; he renounces his freedom because he is afraid of its dangers. This blindness, this deceit, shocks me particularly in writers, whose first virtue—no matter how fantastic their flights—should be a fearless sincerity.

I was in no danger of becoming fascinated with myself, since I had not yet got over the amazement of my good luck. Despite the difficulties of travel, I had already visited many countries, and now I was going to America. If someone awakened my curiosity, in most cases I was able to make his acquaintance. I was a person who received invitations; if I never set foot in any of the *salons,* it was because I had no desire to. To have a good time with people, I need to feel in harmony with them; society women, even the most emancipated ones, were just not my sort; if I had taken part in their rituals, I should have felt bored and guilty. That is why I've never owned an evening dress; I found it repugnant to put on the uniform, not of my sex (I've often worn the sort of clothes that are called very feminine) but of their class. Genet used to complain about the simplicity of my clothes; Simone Berrieau said to me one day: "You don't dress as well as you should!" In Portugal, I had taken pleasure in buying myself a wardrobe; I appreciate lovely things; but the cult of elegance implies a system of values which is foreign to me. Besides which, money could be used for too many things to exempt me from scruples about squandering it on finery.

Money presented problems for me. I respect it because for most people it is hard to earn; when I realized, during the course of that year, that from now on Sartre would have a lot of it, I was alarmed. It was our duty to use it to the best advantage; but how were we to choose among all those who needed it? Along the little roads around La Pouèze, we discussed our new responsibilities uneasily. In fact, we evaded them. Sartre had never taken money seriously, he loathed counting. He had neither the time nor the inclination to turn himself into a philanthropic institution; besides which, there is something unpleasant about charity when it has been carefully thought out. He gave away most of what he earned, but as chance dictated—to friends, to people he met, to people who wrote and asked. I thought it a pity he should be so feckless about his generosity, and I soothed my uneasiness by spending as little as possible on myself. For my tour of America I needed a dress; I bought one at a little place I knew, it was a knit and, I thought, ravishing, but expensive: 25,000 francs.[1] "It's my first concession," I told Sartre, and then burst into tears. My friends laughed at me, but I understand myself. I still imagined—in spite of having demonstrated the opposite in *The Blood of Others*— that there existed a way of not being involved in social injustice, and I thought we were to blame for not trying to find it. In fact, there is no such thing, and in the end I came around to thinking that Sartre's solution was as good as any other. Yet he himself was not satisfied with it, for he found it a burden to be privileged. Our tastes were lower middle class, our style of life continued to be modest. All the same, we did go to restaurants and bars frequented by the wealthy, and we would meet right-wing people in them; it irritated us particularly that we were always running into Louis Vallon. Without

[1] $50.

ever getting used to our new position, little by little—whether for good or for bad—I grew less hesitant about benefiting from it: it was all so contingent, the way the money came and went! Several times I dragged Sartre with me on expensive trips; I yearned for them so deeply, and they gave me so much, that I never blamed myself on that score. On the whole, the way in which I decided to permit myself certain "concessions" and refuse others was decidedly arbitrary; but it seems to me impossible to establish any coherent principle of behavior in this area. I shall come back to this later.

On my return from Holland, I learned that *All Men Are Mortal* had just come out. "My wife likes your last novel very much," the publisher Nagel told me. "Many people think it much inferior to your others, as you know; but she likes it very much." I didn't know. Working on it had been such a pleasure that I had supposed it to be far and away my best. Several of my friends who had read it in manuscript shared this opinion. I had heard (perhaps erroneously) that Queneau had suggested to Gallimard a first printing of 75,000 copies. I had been disconcerted when I learned from Zette that Leiris thought I had used the fantastic too rationally: that's just the reaction of a surrealist, I reassured myself. Nagel's words caught me quite unprepared, and came as something of a shock. But what he had said was soon confirmed. The critics were by no means kind; Rousseaux went so far as to say that he regretted having written about me favorably in the past, and announced that I would never write anything worthwhile again. Among my intimate friends, the book still had its partisans, and also some outside that circle; but after my previous successes it was an indisputable failure. The judgments of certain critics I was unable to reject, and even less so that of the public; such widespread condemnation must mean that I had more or less failed in my attempt. I regretted it, but without being too upset. I still refused to question myself, to torment myself, and I still kept my trust in the future.

CHAPTER III

I WAS NOT PLANNING TO WRITE A book about America, but I wanted to have a good look at it; I knew its literature and, despite my dismaying accent, I spoke English fluently. I had a few friends over there: Stépha, Fernand, Lise. Sartre gave me some addresses. I had dinner with Ellen and Richard Wright, who were getting ready to return to New York before coming back to make their home in Paris.

I went to say good-bye to Olga, who was undergoing treatment at Leysin; she had decided not to stay there very long, boredom was making her lose weight; it was as sinister as Berck; at the end of twenty-four hours I already felt crushed by it. I went back to Paris, and I waited. There were still very few planes making the Atlantic crossing, and that winter was so treacherous they were often forced to turn back in mid-ocean. One evening Sartre finally went with me to the Invalides air terminal and I spent two troubled hours at Orly—the distance, the length of my absence, the magic of America, everything to do with my journey excited and frightened me; and then, suddenly, the plane wasn't going to take off until the following day! I called the Montana and rejoined Sartre and Bost there, but I felt I was nowhere, and all the following day I drifted in limbo. At last I flew away.

In New York I met M. She was about to leave for Paris, where she would remain until my return. She was as charming as Sartre had described her, and she had the prettiest smile in the world.

France was still doing penance, Italy too; Switzerland was insipid. The abundance of luxuries in America bowled me over: the streets, the shop windows, the automobiles, the hairdos and the furs, the bars,

the drugstores, the flashing streams of neon, the distances devoured
by plane, by car, by train, by Greyhound, the shifting splendor of the
landscapes, from the snows of Niagara to the burning deserts of Ari-
zona, and all the different kinds of people with whom I talked
through the long nights and days; I scarcely met any but intellectuals; but all the same what a distance from the cottage cheese salads
of Vassar to the marijuana I smoked in a room at the Plaza with
bohemians from Greenwich Village! One of the fortunate things
about this trip was that, although its general plan was determined by
my lecture program, it left enormous room for chance and inven-
tion; I have related in detail how I profited from this good luck in
America Day by Day.

I was prepared to love America. It was the homeland of capitalism, yes, but it had helped save Europe from Fascism; the atomic
bomb assured it world leadership and freed it from all fear; books
written by certain American liberals had convinced me that a large
section of the nation had a clear and serene awareness of its responsibilities. The reality was a great shock to me. There flourished among
almost all the intellectuals, even those who claimed to be of the Left,
an Americanism worthy of the chauvinism of my father. They approved of all Truman's speeches. Their anti-Communism verged on
neurosis; their attitude toward Europe, toward France, was one of
arrogant condescension. It was impossible to dislodge them, even for
an instant, from their convictions; discussion often seemed to me as
futile as with advanced paranoiacs. From Harvard to New Orleans,
from Washington to Los Angeles, I heard students, teachers and
journalists seriously wondering whether it would not be better to
drop their bombs on Moscow before the U.S.S.R. was in a position to
fight back. It was explained to me that in order to defend freedom it
was becoming necessary to suppress it: the witch-hunt was getting
under way.

What I found most disquieting was the inertia of all these people
ceaselessly nagged by the wildest propaganda. No one, as far as I
know, was talking about the *organization man* yet; but that was
whom I described in my reports, in terms scarcely different from
those used later by American sociologists; they characterized him
above all by his *other-conditioning;* and I was struck by the absence,
even among very young boys and girls, of any interior motivation;
they were incapable of thinking, of inventing, of imagining, of
choosing, of deciding for themselves; this incapacity was expressed by

their conformism; in every domain of life they employed only the abstract measure of money, because they were unable to trust to their own judgment. Another of my surprises was the American woman; even if it is true that the spirit of revenge in her has been exasperated to the point of making her a "praying mantis," she still remains a dependent and relative being; America is a masculine world.[1] These observations, and the importance I granted them, are such that my American experience still remains valid in my eyes today.

All the same, I met a few writers, more or less intimate friends of Richard Wright, with whom I got on very well; they were sincerely pacifist and progressive, and though they were mistrustful of Russia and Stalin, they were free with their criticisms of their own country. And yet they loved so many things about it and taught me to become so attached to it myself that I adopted its history, its literature and its beauties almost as my own. America became still closer to me when I became attached to Nelson Algren toward the end of my stay. Although I related this affair—very approximately—in *The Mandarins*, I return to it now not out of any taste for gossip, but in order to examine more closely a problem that in *The Prime of Life* I took to be too easily resolved: Is there any possible reconciliation between fidelity and freedom? And if so, at what price?

Often preached, rarely practiced, complete fidelity is usually experienced by those who impose it on themselves as a mutilation; they console themselves for it by sublimations or by drink. Traditionally, marriage used to allow the man a few "adventures on the side" without reciprocity; nowadays, many women have become aware of their rights and of the conditions necessary for their happiness: if there is nothing in their own lives to compensate for masculine inconstancy, they will fall a prey to jealousy and boredom. There are many couples who conclude more or less the same pact as Sartre and myself: to maintain throughout all deviations from the main path a "certain fidelity." "*I have been faithful to thee, Cynara, in my fashion.*" Such an undertaking has its risks. It is always possible that one of the partners may prefer a new attachment to the old one, the other partner then considering himself or herself unjustly betrayed; in place of two free persons, a victim and a torturer confront each other.

In certain cases, for one reason or another—children, a common concern, the force of the attachment—the couple is impregnable. If

[1] Eve Merriam, in an article published in 1960 in *The Nation*, has demonstrated that the American male is crushed, not by the female, but by the Organization.

the two allies allow themselves only passing sexual liaisons, then there is no difficulty, but it also means that the freedom they allow themselves is not worthy of the name. Sartre and I have been more ambitious; it has been our wish to experience "contingent loves"; but there is one question we have deliberately avoided: How would the third person feel about our arrangement? It often happened that the third person accommodated himself to it without difficulty; our union left plenty of room for loving friendships and fleeting affairs. But if the protagonist wanted more, then conflicts would break out. On this point, an unavoidable discretion compromised the exact truthfulness of the picture painted in *The Prime of Life*, for although my understanding with Sartre has lasted for more than thirty years, it has not done so without some losses and upsets in which the "others" always suffered. This defect in our system manifested itself with particular acuity during the period I am now relating.

"When you get to Chicago, go and see Algren for me," a young intellectual called Nelly Benson had told me when I was having dinner with her in New York. "He's an amazing man, and a great friend of mine." I have given a faithful account of my first meeting with him in *America Day by Day*, our evening in the lower depths of the city and the following afternoon spent in the bars of the Polish district; but I did not mention the complicity that immediately sprang up between us, nor how disappointed we were not to be able to have dinner together: I was obliged to accept an invitation from two French officials. I called him before I left for the railroad station; they had to take the telephone away from me by force. On the train to Los Angeles I read one of his books and thought about him; he lived in a hovel, without a bathroom or refrigerator, alongside an alley full of steaming trash cans and flapping newspapers; this poverty seemed refreshing, after the heavy odor of dollars in the big hotels and the elegant restaurants, which I had found hard to take. "I'll go back to Chicago," I said to myself; Algren had asked me to, and I wanted to; but if we found this parting painful already, wouldn't the next one hurt us even more? I asked that question in the letter I sent him. "Too bad for us if another separation is going to be difficult," he answered.

The weeks passed; back in New York, friendships grew stronger; one, especially, absorbed a great deal of my time. At the beginning of May, Sartre asked me in one of his letters to postpone my departure because M. was staying another ten days in Paris. Suddenly that made me feel the nostalgia I described Anne as feeling in *The Mandarins:* I'd had enough of being a tourist; I wanted to walk about on the arm of a man who, temporarily, would be mine. I thought first of my New York friend, but he didn't want either to lie to his wife or admit such an affair to her; we decided against it. I called Algren. "Can you come here?" I asked him. He couldn't; but he would like very much to see me in Chicago. I arranged for him to meet me at the airport.

Our first day together was very much like the one Anne and Lewis spent together in *The Mandarins;* embarrassment, impatience, mis-understanding, fatigue, and finally the intoxication of deep under-standing. I stayed in Chicago only three days; I had a great many things to settle in New York; I persuaded Algren to go there with me—it was the first time he'd been in an airplane. I went around arranging things, shopping, saying good-bye; at about five in the afternoon I came back to our room and we stayed with each other until the next morning. People would often talk about him to me; they said he was unstable, moody, even neurotic; I liked being the only one who understood him. If he was sometimes blunt and rude, as people claimed, it was certainly only as a defense. For he possessed that rarest of all gifts, which I should call goodness if the word had not been so abused; let me say that he really cared about people. I told him, before I left him, that my life was permanently fixed in Paris; he believed me without at all understanding what I meant. I promised him we should see each other again, but we did not know when or how, and I arrived in Paris in a dreadful state. Sartre was in trouble, too. Before getting on the boat that brought her to France, M. had written him quite frankly: "I am coming determined to do everything I can to make you ask me to stay." He hadn't asked her to stay. She wanted to prolong her visit until July. Although she had been very friendly with me in New York, she did not really like me. In order to avoid friction, I went with Sartre to live in a little hotel near Port-Royal on the outskirts of Paris; it was almost the country, there were roses in the garden, cows in the meadows, and I worked outside in the sun. We went for walks along the path Jean Racine used to use, overgrown with grass and punctuated with bad alex-andrines. On certain evenings Sartre would go into Paris to meet M. This way of life would have suited me if she had been satisfied with it; but no. The evenings when Sartre stayed out at Saint-Lambert he would receive dramatic telephone calls from her. She could not accept his letting her go away again. But how could he do otherwise? The circumstances were not favorable to compromise solutions. If M. were to make her home in Paris, sacrificing her job, her friendships, everything to which she was accustomed, she would be entitled to expect everything from Sartre; and that was more than he was able to offer. But if he loved her, how could he bear not to see her for months at a time? He listened to her complaints with remorse; he felt that he was to blame. Of course he had warned her there could be no question of his making a life with her. But by saying that he loved her he gave the lie to that warning; for—especially in the eyes of women—love triumphs over every obstacle. M. was not entirely in the wrong. Love's promises express the passion of a moment only; restrictions and reservations are no more binding; in every case, the truth of the present sweeps all pledges imperiously before it. It was natural that M. should think: Things will change. Her mistake was to take for mere verbal precautions what were, with Sartre, less a decision than simply knowledge; and one might conclude that he misled her insofar as it was impossible for him to communicate to her the evidence on which that knowledge was based. Besides which, she, on her side, had not told him that when she began the affair she also rejected its limits. Perhaps he had been thoughtless not to have realized this; his excuse was that, while refusing to alter his relationship with me, he cared for her intensely and wanted to believe that some compromise solution could be found.

Despite the pleasures of the approaching summer, I went through two painful months. At the time, I had swallowed the failure of my last novel, following on that of *Les Bouches Inutiles,* with scarcely a murmur; but underneath, it was still depressing me. All progress had stopped; I had become stagnant. My resolution was insufficient to cut myself off completely from America, and I attempted to prolong my trip by writing a book. I had taken no notes; my long letters to Sartre and a few engagements scribbled in a notebook eked out my memory. This report interested me; but like my essay on Woman—abandoned for the time being—it did not give me what I had always demanded of writing up till then: the feeling of risking and at the same time of transcending myself, an almost religious joy. "I'm just writing a potboiler," I told Sartre. But in any case the pain and the pleasure of writing would not have been enough to settle the memory of my last few days in America. It wouldn't have been impossible to go back to Chicago, since the question of money was no longer crucial; but wouldn't it be better to give up the whole thing? I asked myself that question with an anxiety that bordered on mental aberration. To calm myself, I began to take orthedrine. For the moment, it allowed me to regain my balance; but I imagine that this expedient was not entirely unconnected with the anxiety attacks I suffered from at the time. Since they were founded in reality, my anxiety could at least have been discreet in its manifestations; but it was in fact accompanied by a physical panic that my greatest fits of despair, even when enhanced by alcohol, had never produced. Possibly the war and the period just after it had undermined my health and predisposed me to these paroxysms. Perhaps, too, these crises were a last revolt before resigning myself to age and the end that follows it: I still wanted to separate the shadow from the light. Suddenly I was becoming a stone, and the steel was splitting it: that is hell.

To celebrate my return I gave a party in the *cave* into which the *Lorientais*[1] had moved in the Rue de la Montagne-Sainte-Geneviève. Vian, who was tending bar for me, immediately began to serve the most merciless concoctions; many of the guests sank into a stupor; Giacometti went off to sleep. I was careful and kept going till dawn; I forgot my purse when I left, and went back with Sartre in the afternoon to get it. "And the eye?" the concierge asked us. "Don't you want the eye?" A friend of Vian's, known as the Major, had put his glass eye on the piano and left it there. A month later, in a *cave* in the Rue Dauphine, a place called the Tabou opened, where Anne-Marie Cazalis, a young red-haired poetess who had won the Prix Valéry a few years earlier, received the customers; Vian and his orchestra went to work there and it had an enormous and immediate success. People drank and danced and also brawled a great deal, both inside and out front. The neighborhood declared war on Anne-Marie Cazalis; at night, people threw buckets of water on the customers and even on people just passing by. I didn't go to the Tabou. I didn't see *Gilda*, the film everyone was talking about. I didn't even go to the lecture Sartre gave on Kafka, to raise money for the Ligue Française pour la Palestine Libre.[2] I almost never left Saint-Lambert.

Sartre had kept me in touch with what was happening in his life by letter, and we talked about all the things he had mentioned. He

1 The group Claude Luter had formed.
2 It was at the time of the *Exodus* affair.

had been to see *The Maids* by Genet, which Jouvet had completely misdirected. He had seen Koestler again, intending to give him his *Anti-Semite and Jew* which had just come out; Koestler had stopped him: "I've been to Palestine; I've reached the saturation point about the subject. I must warn you that I won't read your book." Thanks to the intervention of M., who knew Camus, he and Sartre had been reconciled. *The Plague* came out just at that time; here and there, one could still hear the voice that spoke in *The Stranger*. It was Camus' voice and it touched us, but to treat the Occupation as the equivalent of a natural calamity was merely another means of escaping from History and the real problems. Everyone fell in only too easily with the abstract morality expressed by this fable. Shortly after my return, Camus severed his connection with *Combat:* the newspaper strike had seriously affected its financial stability. The paper was refinanced by Smadja and taken over again by Bourdet, who had founded it but who had happened to be in a concentration camp at the time it had been able to come out of clandestinity. In a sense this change was fortunate. *Combat* once more took up a resolutely left-wing position. But Camus had been so closely associated with it that his departure marked for us the end of an epoch.

The new one was not particularly gay. From the moment I landed, I had been struck by how poor France was. Blum's policy—a price and wage freeze—had been a failure; there was not enough coal or grain, the bread ration had been reduced, it was impossible to eat or dress decently without recourse to the black market, and the workers' wages made this impracticable for them. In order to protest against the lowering of their standard of living, 20,000 workers in the Renault factories had gone on strike on April 30th. The food shortage provoked riots and further strikes—stevedores, gas and electricity workers, railroad workers—which Ramadier blamed on an invisible impresario. I learned the extent of the reprisals exacted by the army from the Malgaches: 80,000 dead.[1] And there was fighting in Indochina.[2] At the time of my departure for America, the newspapers were full of stories about the rebellion in Hanoi. It was only when I

[1] In March, they had massacred about 200 European *colons*. The figure of 80,000 was not denied by the government. It was divulged—while the number of victims in the Sétif reprisals remained secret—because the Communists were at present in the opposition.

[2] On March 6, 1946, France had recognized the Republic of Vietnam with Ho Chiminh as its President. But the machinations in Saigon and Bidault's "firmness" had thwarted these agreements.

got back that I discovered it had been provoked by the shelling of
Haiphong: our artillery had killed 6,000 people, men, women and
children. Ho Chi-minh had taken to the bush. The government was
refusing to negotiate, Coste-Floret asserting there were no longer any
military problems in Indochina, while Leclerc was prophesying years
of guerrilla warfare.

The Communist Party had declared its opposition to this war. It
had protested the arrest of the five Malgache members of Parliament.
The Communist ministers supported the Renault strike and left the
government. Meanwhile De Gaulle was talking to Bruneval, and in
Strasbourg he announced the formation of the R.P.F. The class
struggle was coming out into the open, and the odds no longer
favored the proletariat. The bourgeoisie had re-formed its ranks and
the present situation was to its advantage.

This breakup of French unity was, in effect, determined to a
great extent by the collapse of international solidarity. Only two
years had gone by since I had seen newsreels of G.I.s and Russian
soldiers dancing together for joy at Torgau on the banks of the Elbe.
Now, carried away by its own generosity, the United States was planning to make satellites out of all the countries of Europe, including
those in the East. Molotov countered this by rejecting the Marshall
Plan. The Cold War had begun. Even on the Left, very few people
approved of the Communist refusal; among the intellectuals, Sartre
and Merleau-Ponty were almost the only ones who rallied to Thorez's point of view of the "Western trap."

However, the bridges between Sartre and the Communists were
broken. The Party intellectuals attacked him unmercifully because
they were afraid that he would steal their clientele; that his position
was so close to theirs only made them consider him as more dangerous than ever. "You are preventing people from coming to us,"
Garaudy told him. And Elsa Triolet: "You are a philosopher and
therefore an anti-Communist." *Pravda* had spat out insults against
Existentialism that were laughable but none the less painful. Lefebvre had "executed" it in a book praised to the skies by Desanti in
Action, and by Guy Leclerc in *Les Lettres Françaises*. And in *La
Pensée*, Mougin's *La Sainte Famille Existentialiste* had appeared;
also a masterly work of annihilation according to the connoisseurs of
the Communist Party. Garaudy, although he described Sartre as a
"gravedigger of literature," nevertheless kept his insults within the
limits of decency, but Kanapa in *L'Existentialisme n'est pas un*

Humanisme, accused us in the crudest language of being Fascists and "enemies of mankind." Sartre decided to throw off the restraint he had imposed upon himself until then. He collected signatures—those of Pierre Bost, Fombeure, Schlumberger, Mauriac and Guéhenno among others—for a text protesting the calumnies heaped on Nizan, and the press had published it. The C.N.E. had replied and Sartre was going to answer them in the July issue of *Les Temps Modernes.* This break was inevitable since, as he wrote in *What Is Literature?,* which was published at about that time in *Les Temps Modernes: "The policy of Stalin's Communism is incompatible with the honest exercise of a writer's trade."* He took the Communist Party to task for the precedence it gave to scientism, for its oscillations between conservatism and opportunism, and for a utilitarianism which degraded literature to the status of propaganda. Suspect among the bourgeoisie and cut off from the masses, Sartre was condemning himself to a future without a public; from now on he would have merely readers. He accepted this solitude willingly, because it titillated his love of adventure. Nothing could be more despairing than this essay, and nothing more high-spirited. By rejecting him, the Communists were condemning him to political impotence; but since to name is to unmask, and to unmask is to change, Sartre extended his notion of commitment still further and discovered a *praxis* in writing. Reduced to his *petit-bourgeois* singularity, and rejecting it, he was aware of himself as "an unhappy consciousness," but had no taste for jeremiads and was confident of being able to find a way of going beyond this state.

I went to a screening of *The Chips Are Down,* made by Delannoy from a scenario Sartre had written a long while before. Afterward we had supper at the Véfour with Bost and Olga, who had come back from Leysin and was much better. Micheline Presle was brimming with beauty and talent; but Pagliero, whom I had so liked in *Open City*—I had seen it in New York—spoke French with such a bad accent that they had been forced to dub him; the effect was regrettable. And the hero and heroine appeared to be just as dead after their resurrection as before.

In June, the Prix de la Pléiade was awarded (for the last time). The jury's session was a very stormy one, according to Sartre; he succeeded in getting the prize for Genet's plays—*The Maids* and *Deathwatch*—but Lemarchand handed in his resignation. As in preceding years, I was invited to take coffee with the members of the jury. When I went into the dining room, Malraux was speaking and everyone was very quiet; he was talking about *The Plague*. "The question is," he said, "to know whether Richelieu could have written *The Plague*. I say he could. In any case, General de Gaulle *has* written it, it's called *The Edge of the Sword*." He also said, aggressively: "It is so that a Camus can write *The Plague* that men like myself have stopped writing."

Despite its being so late in the season, a theater in London was putting on *The Respectful Prostitute* and *The Victors*. Nagel passed on an invitation to Sartre from the manager; I should have been delighted about it if only he hadn't come with us; being afraid of airplanes, he forced us to make the journey by train, and didn't stop chattering the whole time. In London, he had taken a bizarrely furnished apartment on one side of St. James's Square. We revisited the museums and the streets without him. The blitz, V-1s, V-2s—ruins everywhere; overrun with tall hollyhocks, they made vistas and gardens in the heart of this dense city. Once more, after fifteen years of absence, London won our hearts. I was sorry we were there for only four days.

Nagel had organized a press conference for Sartre; he was stupefied when I said I wasn't going to attend it; then his face suddenly lit up. "Ah!" he said. "That's very clever of you." He couldn't imagine that I merely wanted to go for a walk, and assumed that it was part of a scheme on my part, that I intended to wait until the English journalists put themselves out for *me*. In a setting of overpowering ostentation—antique furniture, Old Masters—we saw the great satrap Alexander Korda. We met a lot of theater people in restaurants and bars. We went to the opening. Laughing, the director said to Sartre: "You've got a surprise coming. . . ." We had indeed; he had cut one whole scene. During the performance, Rita Hayworth, wearing a short, black velvet evening dress and followed by a female companion, made a universally observed entrance—into the auditorium. We had supper with her at the home of a Dutchman. There were only seven or eight people there, and it was a fairly dreary gathering. With her golden shoulders and her magnificent bosom Rita Hayworth was magnificent; but a star without a husband is a sorrier sight than an orphaned child. She spoke charmingly about her past. The Dutchman made some racist observations and she protested. "But all the same, if you had a daughter, would you let her marry a Negro?" he asked. "She'd marry whomever she wanted to," was the reply. The star was certainly no less intelligent than most of the women who don't make their beauty a profession.

Shortly after that, Sartre accompanied M. to Le Havre. She left complaining of the pain he was causing her. She wrote that she would come back either never or for good. In sweltering heat (there had never been such a summer according to the newspapers) we dragged through day after intolerable day in Paris. Pagniez, whom we no longer saw very often but for whom we still had a great deal of affection, told us that his wife was suffering from a blood disease always fatal within two or three years. Sartre was brooding remorsefully. It was a great relief to get into the airplane that took us to Copenhagen. It was cool in that beautiful red and green city. But our first day reminded me of the dark hours when Sartre was followed by lobsters. It was a Sunday, we mingled with the families wading along the sea's edge. Sartre was very quiet, and so was I. I wondered in terror if we had become strangers to one another. Our obsessions melted away little by little during the following days, as we walked among the attractions of the Tivoli and visited the sailors' dives, where we drank *akvavit* late into the night.

In Sweden we disembarked at Helsinborg. After three days along canals and lakes full of flotillas of logs, we reached Stockholm. I loved the city, all glass and water, and also the slow whiteness of the evenings hestitating on the brink of night.

Some Swedish people whom Sartre knew showed us the old streets and restaurants, a charming old theater set among the woods and lakes. One night, when they had taken us out into the country, we saw the aurora borealis. Often I felt they were in the way; how could one be open to things when one was being forced to make polite remarks the whole time? This constraint aggravated the tension inside me which had not completely subsided. I had nightmares. I can remember a yellow eye at the back of my head which was being pierced by a long knitting needle. And my anxiety attacks came back. I tried to conjure these crises away with words:

"The birds are attacking me—must drive them away; it's such an exhausting struggle, keeping them off, day and night: death, our deaths, solitude, vanity; at night, they swoop down on me; in the morning, they take their time flying away. And if something inside my body weakens, there they are, in the flash of a wing. In the café in Stockholm, there were two colors shrieking at one another: orange and green, their meeting was an agony. A hand took me by my scalp;

it pulled, it pulled and my head grew longer and longer as it went on pulling, it was death trying to take me away. Ah! let's put an end to it! I'll pick up a revolver, I'll shoot. I must practice. On rabbits, perhaps, to begin with . . ."

Sartre and I continued north, first by train and then by boat, along a string of lakes. We discovered landscapes that were new to us: dwarf forests, earth the color of amethysts planted with tiny trees red as coral and yellow as gold. They gave me a feeling of childhood and mystery; a troll was bound to pop up at a turn in the path. We did, in fact, see one apparition: a fat woman's extremely white bottom. Two couples were bathing at the foot of a waterfall in nude tranquillity. We left the boat at a peaceful Lapp village; the Lapps were quite short, their faces creased by a fixed smile, and they wore bright blue clothes embroidered in yellow, and sealskin moccasins. The only way a doctor could get there was by the boat we came on, which only called once a week at the most. We stayed several days at Abisko; the hotel was built of wood, and there was a knotted rope in every room so the occupant could climb to safety in case of fire.[1] Around it, there was only the vast forest stretching away on every side, and when I sat there with a book, reindeer would come up to me.

There was no road to Abisko, only the railway; the mailman and the milkman both used the tracks, pedaling up and down on strange vehicles painted bright red. One evening, however, amid all that solitude, the telephone broke the silence; a journalist in Stockholm told Sartre that, because of complaints by neighbors, the police had closed the Tabou for two weeks; did he have any comments? We climbed Mount Njulja and were astonished to find perpetual snow at 45,000 feet and disturbed by the thought that we should never see that spot again; even Sartre, less sensitive than I to the loneliness of things, was moved: that snow-capped landscape of many-colored stones, where dusk melted into dawn, would go on offering itself when our eyes had deserted it forever. One morning we took the train for Narvik. The town had been shelled to bits; its wretchedness was a striking contrast to Swedish opulence. A good example of history laughing in the face of morality.

On our way back, we stopped to visit an old Swedish prince, a lover of literature and the arts, whom Sartre had already met; he was married to a Frenchwoman; they lived in a pretty house amid

---

1 The hotel was destroyed by fire two years later, in 1949.

peaceful valleys, and were full of wonder at their good fortune. "We too will have a happy old age!" I said to myself as I sipped a glass of old akvavit, aged in little wooden casks; I must have been even more shaken up than I actually recall to have taken refuge in such a far-off, well-behaved dream; but the fact is that it put the finishing touch to my convalescence and I returned to France with my mind completely calm again.

I left again immediately; I had decided to return to Chicago in the middle of September. I had sent a cable to Algren asking him if he agreed; he did. I got on a T.W.A. plane taking some Greek peasants and tradespeople from Athens to America. It was a terrible old crate which flew at a ceiling limit of about six or seven thousand feet, and took twelve hours to get from Shannon to the Azores. I went to sleep during that part of the journey and woke with a start. The plane was turning around; a motor had just given out and we were going back to Shannon. I was scared for the next five hours without a break; I read science-fiction stories, escaping for the minutes to another planet or into prehistory, only to find myself back over the ocean: if another motor gave out, I would disappear into it. Ah! how I longed for death to come to me disguised, without inflicting its imminence and, above all, its loneliness! Around me, no one turned a hair. But what a sudden explosion of talk as soon as the plane was on the ground! A bus took us a long way away, to the edge of a fjord where there was a mock village that belonged to the airport; everyone had a little house to himself with a peat fire burning in it. I stayed there two days, dragging myself along roads whose signposts and notices bore indecipherable words, I sat on the soft slopes of ash-green meadows laced with low walls of gray stones. In the bar I drank Irish whisky while I read Algren's first novel which told me all about his childhood. I was no longer sure that he existed, or Chicago either, or Paris. We set out again; when the plane landed in the Azores, a tire burst and I had to wait another eighteen hours in the airport concourse. Then we flew through storms; the plane fell nearly 5,000 feet from cloud to cloud. When we arrived, I ached all over, in body and soul. It seemed as though the customs officials would never finish evaluating the miles of lace that the Greeks were dragging about in their suitcases; when I came out, Algren was not there, and I thought I was never going to find him again.

He had been waiting for me for four days in the house on Wabansia Avenue, and the moment we looked at each other again, I knew I had been right to come back.

It was during these two weeks that I discovered Chicago:[1] the prisons, the police stations and the lineups, the hospitals, the stockyards, the burlesque houses, the slums with their empty lots and their nettles. I saw very few people. Some of Algren's friends worked in radio and television, though they were finding it pretty hard to keep their jobs; the Communist purge was spreading panic in Hollywood, and all over the United States liberals were being thought of as Reds. The rest were dope addicts, gamblers, whores, thieves, ex-convicts or outlaws; they were all escapees from American conformism; that is why Algren liked to be around them; but they were not particularly friendly. He was writing about them in the novel he was working on at the time. I read a first draft of it, typed on yellow paper and covered with crossouts. I also read Algren's favorite authors: Vachel Lindsay, Sandburg, Masters, Stephen Benét, all old rebels who had defended America against what she was now becoming. I reread newspapers and magazines to fill in the gaps in my reportage.

Again Algren asked me to stay with him for good, and I explained that this was impossible. But we parted less sadly than in May, because in the spring I was to return so that we could take a trip together lasting several months, down the Mississippi and then to Guatemala and Mexico.

In July, De Gaulle had called the Communists separatists and the Communist Party "public enemy Number One." The French bourgeoisie was already dreaming of preventive war. They were having a fine time reading books by Koestler and Kravchenko, and other works of the sort written by repentant Communists.

I met a certain number of these converts, and they astonished me by the lyric ecstasy of their hatred. None of them proposed an analysis of the U.S.S.R. or offered any constructive criticism; they were content to grind out romantic novelettes. Communism, for them, was a world-wide Blot, a Conspiracy, a Fifth Column, a sort of Ku Klux Klan. The hysteria in their eyes was an accusation of the regime that had put it there; but it was impossible to establish any connection between their exotic stories and the lies of the Stalinist government. They were almost maniacally suspicious

[1] In *America Day by Day*, I amalgamated this second visit with the first.

of one another, and each considered those who had left the Party later than himself to be criminals.

There was another category which we found equally unpleasant: the sympathizers at all costs. "As far as I'm concerned," said one of them proudly, "the Communists can give me as many kicks in the ass as they want; they still won't discourage me." Faced with even the most disturbing facts—at that time, the hanging of Petkov—they simply closed their eyes: "You have to believe in something, after all." For us, the U.S.S.R. was the country which embodied socialism, but also one of the two Great Powers hatching a new war; no doubt Russia didn't want it; but she was accepting it as inevitable, preparing for it, and thereby putting the world in danger. A refusal to side with the U.S.S.R. was not a negative attitude, as Sartre had affirmed in *What Is Literature?* By eluding the alternative between the two blocs, he was making the decision to invent another way out.

One of his old colleagues, called Bonafé, knew Ramadier well and suggested to him that we should be entrusted with a radio program to express our views; Sartre accepted. We did not wish to be dependent on the *Présidence du Conseil;* the *Temps Modernes* hour was attached to the "literary and dramatic programs" department. The first week, Sartre—with the help of a group of friends including myself—urged his listeners to reject the Cold War politics of the two blocs. To become part of either one or the other would only aggravate the conflict between them; he declared that peace was possible and censured the editors of *France-Dimanche* for leaving their front-page headline space blank in one of their recent issues because they could not bring themselves to print the words they felt were necessary: "War before Christmas."

The day after the triumphant victory of the R.P.F. in the cantonal elections, we used our program to attack De Gaulle. Following the method used by Pascal in his *Provincial Letters,* we demolished—*we* being Sartre, Bonafé, Merleau-Ponty, Pontalis and myself—the arguments of a psuedo-Gaullist played by Chauffard; all the arguments we put in his mouth were taken from the R.P.F. newspapers, and we had been quite explicit that the character was being played by an actor; we were accused of trickery nevertheless. Bonafé was blamed for being too violent, which unfortunately was true; but in any case we aroused a great deal of indignation; the press gave us the mudslinging of our lives. Bénouville and Torrès insisted that Sartre continue the discussion with them, on the air. He accepted; but they were probably afraid he would settle their hash too easily; leaving Sartre in one of the radio building offices, they got together in another for a consultation and, when they came back, said they had thought it over and decided that because Sartre had gone too far they refused to hold a public discussion with him. Aron had accompanied Bénouville, with whom he was in agreement. This attitude brought to a head the quarrel which had been brewing between Sartre and him ever since he began writing for *Figaro* and sympathizing with the R.P.F.

Our discussion of the Communist Party was broadcast two weeks later. Forced out of the government, attacked by the Socialists and hated by the bourgeoisie, the Communists were in a state of isolation scarcely calculated to make them flexible; nevertheless, Sartre had been officially asked, at Hervé's instigation, to take the initiative in the formation of anti-Fascist "vigilante committees." We portioned out our criticisms and reservations in such a way as to make the common struggle possible. But in vain. The program inspired by Hervé was revoked, and he tore us to pieces. We recorded several other conversations: an interview with Rousset, just back from Germany; a discussion of what the Right called the "sordid materialism" of the masses. But on December 3rd, when Schumann replaced Ramadier, he suppressed our program immediately.

While Schumann was busy trying to create a "third force," prices rose 51 percent and wages only 19 percent. Ramadier suppressed the coal subsidy; there was an immediate jump of 40 percent in the price of coal, gas, electricity and transportation. In the mines around Paris and Marseilles, strikes broke out which turned into riots when Schumann attempted to pass an antistrike law; railroads were sabotaged; the miners fought with the C.R.S. sent by Moch to guarantee "the freedom to work." Nevertheless, the unity of the trade unions was broken; the number of strikers fell from three million to one million, F.O. broke away from the C.G.T.; the working class found itself in too weakened a state to be able to prevent the Marshallization of France.

A few Socialists—Marceau-Pivert, Gazier—seeking to constitute an opposition within the S.F.I.O., solicited the support of those men of the Left who did not belong to any party; they would draw up together an appeal in favor of peace and the creation of a neutral and socialist Europe. We met every week at Izard's home: Rousset, Merleau-Ponty, Camus, Breton and a few others. We argued over every word, every comma. In December, the text was finally signed by *Esprit, Les Temps Modernes,* Camus, Bourdet, Rousset, and published in the press. Camus and Breton then brought up the problem of the death penalty; they demanded its abolition as a political measure. Many of us thought on the contrary, that it was only as a political measure that it could be justified. The group dispersed.

There were other points of dissension between Camus and ourselves; politically, at all events, we still had some things in common; he had an aversion for the R.P.F.; he had quarreled (or was preparing to do so) with Ollivier, who had espoused Gaullism and was writing for *Carrefour*. Camus was less free, less intimate with us than he had once been, but our friendship still subsisted. On the other hand, we broke with Koestler during that winter.

At first he was very friendly toward us. I was working in the Flore one autumn morning; he came in with Mamaine and said: "Shall we go have a glass of white wine?" I followed them to a neighboring bistro; as we stood at the counter, he asked: "We're going to the Jeu de Paume. Would you like to come with us?" "Why not?" I said. They laughed. "We appear, you're free; you're always free, it's marvelous." They were happy to be back in Paris again, and it was pleasant looking at the paintings with them. Koestler examined the large photographs exhibited on the ground floor and squinted slyly. "You see? All the painters with great handsome heads, all the ones with the faces of geniuses, are quite mediocre. Whereas Cézanne and Van Gogh have little heads, no faces at all . . . like Sartre and me." I found such childish vanity almost touching. I was a bit more embarrassed when he asked in his knowing tone: "How many copies did they print of *The Plague*? Eighty thousand? That's not too bad . . ." and he reminded us that *Arrival and Departure* had sold 200,000 copies.

When I saw him again with Sartre, we found him much gloomier and more excitable than the year before. He was worried about the success of his latest book, which had just appeared in London. He was always going to the desk of the Pont-Royal to see if his publisher had sent him any press clippings. The occupation forces had withdrawn from Italy, where preparations were getting under way for the first elections. He was sent to report on them by an English newspaper, and came back convinced that they would be a triumph for the Communists; the French Communist Party would then take heart, seize power, and the whole of Europe would speedily fall into

Stalin's hands. Excluded from such a future himself, he intended to forbid it to all his contemporaries: the very mechanisms of thought would be overthrown. He believed in telepathy; it was a means of communication due to develop in a way that would defy all expectations. His "catastrophism" expressed itself in headaches, fits of lethargy and black moods.

He wanted to repeat our night at the Schéhérézade. We went with him, Mamaine, Camus, Sartre and myself—Francine wasn't there—to another Russian nightclub. He insisted on letting the *maître d'hôtel* know that he was being accorded the honor of waiting on Camus, Sartre and Koestler. In a tone more hostile than the year before, he returned to the theme of "No friendship without political agreement." As a joke, Sartre was making love to Mamaine, though so outrageously one could scarcely have said he was being indiscreet, and we were all far too drunk for it to be offensive. Suddenly, Koestler threw a glass at Sartre's head and it smashed against the wall. We brought the evening to a close; Koestler didn't want to go home, and then he found he'd lost his wallet and had to stay behind in the club; Sartre was staggering about on the sidewalk and laughing helplessly when Koestler finally decided to climb back up the stairway on all fours. He wanted to continue his quarrel with Sartre. "Come on, let's go home!" said Camus, laying a friendly hand on his shoulder; Koestler shrugged the hand off and hit Camus, who then tried to hurl himself on his aggressor; we kept them apart. Leaving Koestler in his wife's hands, we all got into Camus' car; he too was suitably soused in vodka and champagne, and his eyes began to fill with tears: "He was my friend! And he hit me!" He kept collapsing onto the steering wheel and sending the car into the most terrifying swerves and we would try to haul him up completely sobered by our fear. During the next few days we often went back to that night together; Camus would ask us perplexedly: "Do you think it's possible to go on drinking like that and still work?" No. And in fact such excesses had become very rare for all three of us; they had had some meaning when we were still refusing to believe that our victory had been stolen from us; now, we knew where we stood.

Koestler was now declaring that the best solution for France at that time, all things considered, was Gaullism. He had several arguments with Sartre. One day, when I happened to be in the bar of the Pont-Royal with Violette Leduc, he came up to me with a member of the R.P.F. in tow. The latter immediately attacked me point-blank:

publicly, Sartre was opposing De Gaulle; but the Rassemblement had contacted him, made him offers that would be very worth his while, and, in sum, he had promised to support the movement. I shrugged my shoulders. The Gaullist refused to let the matter rest and I grew heated; Koestler listened to us with a smile on his lips. "All right! Make a bet on it," he said. "I'll be witness to it. Whoever is in the wrong will buy a bottle of champagne." At that I left. When Sartre challenged him about his attitude, Koestler replied laughingly that one should always be prepared for anything from anyone, and that I had taken the matter too seriously. "It's just a woman's squabble!" he ended up, unsuccessfully trying to trap Sartre into a male complicity. He left Paris; when he returned shortly afterward, he ran into us outside the Pont-Royal and asked: "When are we going to see each other?" Sartre got out his notebook, then changed his mind. "We haven't got anything to say to each other any more." "But we're not going to quarrel over our political opinions!" said Koestler, with an inconsistency that left us temporarily speechless. Sartre put his notebook back in his pocket. "When people's opinions are so different, how can they even go to a film together?"[1] And that was how things remained between us. A few weeks later, we read two articles in *Carrefour—Où Va la France?*—in which Koestler accused the French Communist Party of secretly preparing for civil war. He was hoping for, and predicted, the triumph of Gaullism.

Sartre's enemies continued to add fuel to the flames of the ambiguities that had been created around Existentialism. The Existentialist label had been applied to all our books—even our prewar ones—and to those of our friends, Mouloudji's among others; also to a certain style of painting and a certain sort of music. Anne-Marie Cazalis had the idea of profiting by this vogue. She belonged, like Vian and a few others, both to the literary world of Saint-Germain-des-Prés and to the subterranean world of jazz. While talking to some journalists, she baptized the clique of which she was the center, and the young people who prowled between the Tabou and the Pergola, as Existentialists. The press, and particularly *Samedi-Soir*, which had a financial interest in her success, gave the Tabou a tremendous amount of publicity. No week passed during that fall of 1947 in which something wasn't printed about the brawls and festivities of its

[1] Koestler, when he wrote about this episode, erroneously attributed the initiative for breaking off our relationship to me.

habitués, writers, journalists and politicians. Anne-Marie Cazalis was only too delighted to be photographed and interviewed, and people also began to be interested in her friend, the plump Toutoune, who had become a beautiful young girl with long black hair: Gréco. At Agnès Capri's Gaieté-Montparnasse, she had played the part of the farting girl in Vitrac's *Victor, ou les Enfants au Pouvoir*. She wore the new "Existentialist" uniform. The musicians from the various *caves* and their fans had been down to the Côte d'Azur during the summer and brought back the new fashion imported from Capri—itself originally inspired by the Fascist tradition—of black sweaters, black shirts and black pants.

Anne-Marie Cazalis had seemed very pleasant when I had seen her in the Flore at the time she was awarded her prize. She and Astruc were very attached to each other; Bost was quite friendly with her and said she was very intelligent and remarkably cultivated; she was of Protestant upbringing, and the reserve of both her manners and her conversation was in striking contrast to the effect she had made on the tradespeople of the district. However, I had a grudge against her because it was she who had written most of the article in *France-Dimanch* on the "Sartre Scandal." While we were out one evening with Herbaud, he said he wanted to go down to the Tabou. The place was so noisy, crowded and smoky, that we could hardly hear each other or even breathe. Nevertheless we sat at the corner of a table with Anne-Marie Cazalis and managed to chat; she proved to be both funny and very sharp-witted, manipulating ellipsis, litotes, and allusion with great dexterity. She defended herself about the "Sartre Scandal" and ended up: "In fact, it was Astruc who was to blame." I was very fond of Astruc and this piece of perfidy flabbergasted me. We let the matter drop, and the conversation came to an end. Every time I have seen Anne-Marie Cazalis since, I have appreciated her sharp-witted charm, but she carried gossip to the point of tactlessness.

Sartre, who loved youth and jazz, was irritated by the attacks on the "Existentialists"; wandering about, dancing, listening to Vian play the trumpet—where was the harm in that? All the same, they were used to discredit him. What confidence could one have in a philosopher whose teachings inspired orgies? How could one believe in the political sincerity of a "master thinker" whose disciples lived for nothing more than having a good time? There was even more gossip about him than in 1944-45, but of a far more unpleasant sort; the Resistance press had not been able to weather the storm, and we had seen the return of professional journalism which was prepared to stoop to anything. During a big dinner he gave on his return from America, at the time when he was preparing to take over *France-Soir* again, Lazareff said publicly: "I'll have Existentialism's scalp." He wasn't the only one after it. But to demolish Sartre, they had to talk about him; so much so that the press itself was creating all the publicity it was accusing him of seeking. Between a venomous report of his broadcast on Gaullism and another, equally ill-intentioned, on a debate about him by some theologians, they described a typical evening at the Tabou, of which, according to them, he was one of the pillars.[1] They churned out a thousand unpleasant or ridiculous details about him, all categorically false—for example, the pearl-gray hat, contrasting with the sloppiness of his suits, that he was supposed to have replaced every month out of vanity, during the period when he was teaching. Sartre had never at any time worn a hat. The stares directed at us in public places were already soiled with this dirt, and I no longer enjoyed going out much any more.

We spent the Christmas holidays at La Pouèze. Mme Lemaire thought Sartre's political views extreme, and we suspected her of voting for the M.R.P. She was against free education (scholarships were quite enough), against Social Security (it would be abused), and against union minimum wages (in the name of the freedom to work). But we attached no more importance to her political opinions than she did to ours. We were always happy to see her, both for her own sake and because she was a link with our lost past. Pagniez, as I have said, had moved far away from us. Marco had gone completely out of our lives; at the end of the war, an unhappy love affair, the frustration of his ambitions, his baldness and his obesity had sent him half mad. He used to weep buckets of tears over Sartre, who still visited him devotedly every week. A psychiatrist gave him a series of electric-shock treatments. He stopped weeping but began to hate the people around him. He spread the rumor that Mme Lemaire was a poisoner, and also that I had stolen his library. He still came to see her, but less and less frequently.[2] During this stay, I went on with my essay on Woman. Sartre let his mind wander, then began work on a new play, *Red Gloves*.

In February, we were invited to Berlin for the opening of *The Flies*. "Above all," said Sperber, when we ran into him about that

[1] We have been there twice.
[2] He died in an automobile accident in Algeria, in 1957.

time, "don't set foot in the Soviet Zone: a car draws up to the side-walk, a door opens, they pull you in; no one ever sets eyes on you again."

I felt very uneasy getting on the train to Berlin. The idea of seeing Germans and talking to them was painful. But there it was! I had been taught, once, that to remember is to forget; time passed for everyone, for me as well. As soon as I set foot in Berlin I found my bitterness disarmed. Everything was in ruins; so many cripples and so much poverty! Alexanderplatz, Unter den Linden, everything had been smashed to pieces. Huge stone doorways without doors opened onto kitchen gardens, balconies dangled crookedly across the façades of buildings that were nothing but façades. As Claudine Chonez had written in *Les Temps Modernes,* an umbrella and a sewing machine on top of an operating table here would not have seemed at all out of place; the premises themselves seemed to have no premise any more. To cultivate a derangement of the senses, as Rimbaud suggested, would have been superfluous; reality itself was an insanity. And I walked in flesh and blood through that legendary nightmare: Hitler's Chancellery.

We were living in the French Zone, in the residential quarter where a few villas were still standing. We took our meals at the Cultural Attaché's, in private homes or in clubs. Once, armed with coupons we tried to eat in an ordinary restaurant; all we got was a bowl of bouillon. We talked to some students; no books, not even in the libraries; nothing to eat, the cold, journeys of one or two hours every day, and an agonizing question: We didn't do anything, is it fair that we have to pay?

The problem of punishment was troubling all the Germans. Some of them—mostly those on the Left—thought they should keep the memory of their errors alive forever; this was the theme of the film *Murderers Among Us* made in the Russian Zone. Others submitted to their present misfortunes with bitterness in their hearts. The censorship prevented them from speaking out; the various publications and the theaters avoided the problem by playing off the different zones against each other: the Americans allowed them to laugh at the Russians, the Russians at the Americans. We went to a revue full of sinister humor, which was a satire on this Occupation.

We were disconcerted by the production of *The Flies;* the play had been staged in an expressionist style in settings reminiscent of Hell. The temple of Apollo looked like the inside of a bunker. I didn't think it was very well acted, however, the audience applauded enthusiastically because the play urged them to rid themselves of their guilt. In his lectures—which I didn't attend, preferring to wander about among the ruins—Sartre repeated that it was better to build a future than to lament over the past.

We had walked into the Soviet sector without even being aware that we had done so, and no car drove up to kidnap us, but two Russians whom we met at the Cultural Attaché's proved to be as cold as ice toward us. At a private screening of *Murderers Among Us*, there was no one to receive us—neither the director, nor the theater manager. However, Sartre didn't think this was any reason—the contrary in fact—to play along with the Americans who were trying to monopolize him; he agreed to attend only one private dinner given by an American woman who wanted him to meet some German writers. When we were ushered in, we found ourselves in a room with about two hundred other people; we had fallen right into the trap: instead of having dinner, Sartre was obliged to answer questions. Anna Seghers happened to be there, so radiant with her white hair, her intense blue eyes and her smile that she almost reconciled me to the idea of growing old. She didn't agree with Sartre. "We need to feel guilt, we Germans, right now," she said emphatically. Sartre was taken aside by a Marxist called Stainiger who had recently described him in an S.E.P. newspaper as being an agent of American capitalism; he replied to this charge and Stainiger more or less accepted his reasoning. As a result of that evening, we were invited to lunch in a Soviet club, and this time the Russians thawed slightly— very slightly. Sartre was placed between a Russian woman and a German woman who asked him to sign one of his books for her; he did so and then turned to his other neighbor feeling slightly embarrassed. "I expect you find it silly, writing dedications in books. . . ." "I don't see why," she said, and tore off a piece of the paper tablecloth; but her husband gave her a meaningful look and she crumpled it up. Germany, by the time we had left, had made a very lugubrious impression on us. We were very far from foreseeing the "miracle" that was to transform it several months later.

Misrahi, who was a member of the Stern group, had been arrested for possession of arms and immured in the Santé prison. On February 15th, Sartre gave evidence on his behalf; Misrahi had the full sympathy of both the court and the public. When

Sartre gave it as his opinion that the defendant had been a good student, the judge interrupted him. "Good? Do you mean excellent?" "Certainly," replied Sartre, realizing that he must depart from his usual moderation of tone. Misrahi got off with a 12,000-franc fine. Betty Knout attended the trial.

It was at about this time that Altmann and Rousset had a long debate with Sartre. Of all the people we had met at Izard's, David Rousset was, if not the most interesting, at least the most voluminous. Merleau-Ponty had been in contact with him before the war, when Rousset was a Trotskyite; he described him to us when he got back after being deported: a frail skeleton drifting about in a Japanese bathrobe, he weighed less than 90 pounds. When Merleau-Ponty introduced us to him, Rousset had regained his corpulence; one eye was covered with a black patch, and he had several teeth missing; he had the look of a pirate and the voice of a megaphone. The first thing of his we had read was his essay on *L'Univers Concentrationnaire,* in *La Revue Internationale,* then *Les Jours de Notre Mort;* I admired the will to live that illuminated all his accounts and stories. Taking his inspiration from the "appeal" drawn up at Izard's, he was working with Altmann, Jean Rous, Boutbien, Badiou, Rosenthal and several others to start a *"Rassemblement démocratique et révolutionnaire"* that would draw together all the various Socialist forces not aligned with Communism and use them to construct a Europe independent of the two blocs. There were many movements fighting for a united Europe; the "Estates-General of Europe" was due to be convened in The Hague during May. But the idea of Rousset's group, the R.D.R., was that the union should be formed at the level of basic principles and from a Socialist and neutralist point of view. It was hoped that Sartre would play a part on the executive committee. I was afraid he would simply waste a lot of time in such an enterprise; we had already wasted so much at Izard's! He told me he could scarcely preach commitment and then avoid it when he was offered the chance. The creation of the Kominform and then, on February 25th, the *"coup"* in Prague, aggravated both anti-Communism and the general war psychosis. Americans began canceling trips to Europe. In France, though no one began packing to leave, there was much talk of a Russian invasion. Sartre believed that between a Communist Party aligned with the U.S.S.R. and an S.F.I.O. that had sold out to the bourgeoisie there was still room for action on our part. He therefore signed a manifesto in which he associated himself with Rousset and his comrades and, on March 10th, gave a lecture in which he developed the theme "War is not inevitable." On March 19th, he called a meeting in the Salle Wagram; an enormous number of people attended, and the movement began to collect adherents. Bourdet didn't become a member, but he supported it in his articles while launching a campaign in *Combat* for peace and European unity. Notwithstanding this support, the R.D.R. still needed a newspaper of its own. Sartre rather expected Altmann to make the *Franc-Tireur* into the mouthpiece of the movement, since, with Rousset, he was one of its founders. He refused to do so; it was necessary to make do with a bi-monthly called *La Gauche R.D.R.* whose first issue appeared in May and was not particularly scintillating: there was a shortage of funds. That was also the reason, according to Rousset, why the R.D.R. was getting off to such a slow start; but he had an infectious confidence in the future. However, in his speech at Compiègne in March, De Gaulle redoubled the violence of his attacks on the Communists; an enormous R.P.F. congress was held at Marseilles in April. The Americans were demanding that Joliot-Curie be dismissed from the Atomic Control Commission. Gasperi carried off the victory in the Italian elections. To oppose such a Right while keeping the necessary distance from Stalinism was not an easy task. Sartre gave an account of his attitude in the *Entretiens* with Rousset, which appeared first in *Les Temps Modernes* and subsequently in book form.

All the reasons he gave for his adherence to the R.D.R. were merely objective ones; but why had he felt the need to enter a movement which (in principle at least) was of such a militant nature? He gave some indications of the answer to this question in some unpublished notes written several years later: *"My deepest idea at the time: all one can do is to bear witness to a way of life which is doomed to disappear but which will later be reborn; and perhaps the best works will testify to this way of life in the future and so be a way of permitting its preservation. One vacillates, then, between the adoption of an ideological position and action. But if I advocate an ideological position, immediately people begin urging me into action. What is Literature?* led me into the R.D.R."

He consented to this shift because he himself had found a new relation, born of the hatred he had provoked: *"Good effects of hatred. To feel oneself hated; an element of culture."* At first, he had been appalled by it; in the very name of bourgeois humanism and the democratic ideal, he was with the masses; and they were against him! But if God does not exist, the judgment of the other is the absolute: *"The hatred of others reveals my objectivity to me."* Whereas before he reacted to the situation in all innocence, without thought for himself, he now knew that it enveloped his reality for others; he was now forced to regain that objectivity, to set it, in other words, in agreement with his inner decision. *"From '47 on, I had a double principle of reference: I also judged my principles in relation to those of others—those of Marxism."* This implies that he could not rest content believing himself to be right subjectively. He refused to tolerate *being* an enemy of the oppressed; he had to transform his relation to them by contributing to the modification of both the internal and the international situation. It was necessary to take part in an action.

"Let us suppose that this contradiction of which I am an example (torn between bourgeoisie and proletariat), and which I now know to be characteristic of our time, instead of representing a freedom, a positive content, is merely the expression of a very specific and limited way of life (that of the socialistic bourgeois intellectual). What if it were to disappear without a trace in the future? In short, I fluctuate between this first idea: that my privileged position affords me the means of making a synthesis of formal liberties and material liberties; and this second idea: that my contradictory position affords me no liberty at all! It gives me an unhappy consciousness, and there's an end of it. In the second case, what disappears is my transcendence. I merely reflect my own situation. All my political efforts are directed toward finding a group that will give a meaning to my transcendence, that will prove by its existence (European R.D.R.) that my contradictory position was the true one.

"If I am wrong, however, my situation is one of those in which synthesis is impossible. Even my attempt to transcend myself is rendered false. In that case, I must renounce the optimistic idea that one can be a man in any situation. An idea inspired by the Resistance: even under torture one could be a man. But it was not there that the problem lay; it lay in the fact that certain situations are perfectly livable but made intolerably false by objective contradictions.

"The R.D.R. for me:

"(1) Middle classes and proletariat (I cannot comprehend the non-Communist proletariat choosing the bourgeoisie. It has a different structure).

"(2) *Europe. Not America, not the U.S.S.R., but the intermediary between them (therefore a bit of both).*

"(3) *Democratic and material liberties. At bottom, I wanted to resolve the conflict without* transcending *my own situation. . . ."*

The uneasiness that had induced Sartre to enter the R.D.R. also led him to an ideological reconsideration. He worked assiduously for two years confronting dialectic with history and morality with *praxis,* in the hope of reaching a synthesis between *doing* and *being* which would preserve strictly ethical values.

We were working less on the magazine than in the years just past. To all intents and purposes, it was Merleau-Ponty who ran it. People claimed that I was the author of the *Vie d'une Prostituée* we published in it; it was certainly beyond my powers to produce that astonishing piece of raw writing. Marie-Thérèse existed, and it was she herself who wrote down these memories in a single spurt, before returning to her old profession as a nurse.

We went out very little now. The day *Paris 1900* was presented there was a general transportation strike, and we went to it in a *fiacre.* Nicole Vedrès had done her work well; she blew the myth of *la belle époque* to bits. Thanks to Gérard Philipe and Micheline Presle, the movie of *Devil in the Flesh* which we saw at a private screening seemed to us not unworthy of Radiguet's novel. Among the new Italian movies, we were already familiar with *Open City, Shoeshine* and *Four Steps in the Clouds;* but *Paisan,* especially the episode in the reeds, filmed by Rossellini, was far and away the best of them all. From America we had *The Grapes of Wrath.* Dullin put on Salacrou's *Archipel Lenoir.* He had been put out of the Sarah-Bernhardt and no longer had a theater of his own, so it was at the Théâtre Montparnasse that he created the role of the old satyr of a grandfather. We also went to the Marigny to see Barrault's production of *Occupe-toi d'Amélie.* At the Orangerie, we saw the Turner exhibition. From time to time we went to hear a concert. Sartre was beginning to develop a taste for Schönberg and Berg.

He turned his mind to getting *Red Gloves* put on. The subject of the play had been suggested to him by the assassination of Trotsky. I had known one of Trotsky's ex-secretaries in New York; he told me how the murderer, having managed to get himself hired as Trotsky's secretary, had lived for a long time by his victim's side in a house fanatically well guarded. Sartre had pondered on this dead-end situation; he had imagined a young Communist, born into the middle classes, seeking to erase his origin by an act, but unable to tear himself away from his subjectivity, even at the price of an assassination; in opposition to him he had created a militant politician utterly devoted to his objectives. (Once again, the confrontation of morality and *praxis*.) As he said in his interviews, Sartre had no intention of writing a political play. It became one simply because he had chosen members of the Communist Party as its protagonists. The play didn't seem to me to be anti-Communist. The Communists were presented as the only valid force against the Regent and the bourgeoisie; if a leader, in the interests of the Resistance, of socialism, of the masses, had another leader suppressed, it seemed to me as it did to Sartre that he was exempt from all judgment of a moral order. It was war, he was fighting; this did not mean that the Communist Party was made up of assassins. And then—just as in *The Victors* the arrogant and egocentric Henri is morally dominated by the Greek Communist—so in *Red Gloves* Sartre's sympathy went to Hoederer. Hugo decides to kill in order to prove that he is capable of doing so, without knowing if Louis is in the right against Hoederer. Afterward he decides to take credit for this irresponsible act when his comrades order him to keep quiet. He is so fundamentally in the wrong that the play could be put on, during a period of thaw, in a Communist country; which is in fact what happened in Yugoslavia recently. Only, in the Paris of 1948, circumstances were different.

Sartre realized this and knew what to expect. His adherence to the R.D.R. had earned him a new series of attacks. In February, there appeared on the *Pique-Feu* page of *Action* several anonymous and sickening insinuations about our private life. *Les Lettres Françaises* printed *Le Génie de Six Heures*, in which Magnane had sketched a heavily distorted and scarcely recognizable portrait of Sartre which one could only despise. Meanwhile Kanapa was pulling *Situations I* to pieces. Elsa Triolet was writing a book and lecturing in an attempt to instigate a boycott of the filthy writings of Sartre, Camus and Breton; my sister had heard her speak publicly against Sartre in Belgrade with the deepest hatred in her voice. The situation could scarcely have been any worse.

Simone Berriau accepted *Red Gloves* without hesitation; the parts of Hoederer and Jessica were given to Luguet and Marie Olivier; but who could play Hugo? Names were suggested and discarded. One afternoon, at the Véfour, Berriau suddenly said: "I know it sounds stupid but—why don't we try Perrier?" We had imagined

Hugo as thin and tormented; but anyway, all right, we might as well try it. From the very first rehearsals, Perrier triumphed: he *was* Hugo, just as Vitold had been Garcin in *No Exit*. The direction was assigned to Valde, and amicably supervised by Cocteau; Bérard came round to give advice about the sets; there was always a smell of ether floating around his beard. I was enchanted by the language of these theater folk. At first, Luguet gave his militant Communist too much drawing-room comedy. "You know," Cocteau told him, "you're utterly charming, you drip charm; so don't *try* to be charming; on the contrary, try *not* to be charming; if you don't, what you come up with will be quite extraordinary, but the character won't come out true." "In fact, you think I have no talent," Luguet answered grumpily. There was one line in the play that irritated him. "He's vulgar," Jessica says to Hugo. Sartre explained it: she's lying in order to conceal the interest Hoederer arouses in her. "Oh well! If you suppose the audience will think I'm vulgar, you're within your rights I suppose," was Luguet's last word.

Sartre wasn't there on opening night. (He was giving a lecture to a Masonic Lodge, certain Masons having assured him that their organization could give serious support to the efforts of the R.D.R.: he saw, he heard, he understood.) All the actors were perfect; the newspapers announced next day that Perrier was a new Guitry. I was in a box with Bost, and people came up and shook our hands. "Magnificent! Wonderful!" However, the bourgeois critics did not announce their verdict straight off; they waited to see what the Communists would say. The Communists spat it out like tainted meat. "For 30 pieces of silver and a mess of American pottage, Jean-Paul Sartre has sold out what remained of his honor and probity," wrote one Russian critic. The bourgeoisie immediately buried Sartre in bouquets. One afternoon, on the terrace of the Rhumerie Martiniquaise, Claude Roy was going by and stopped to shake my hand; he had never stooped to using low methods against Sartre. "It was really too bad," I told him, "that you Communists didn't take over *Red Gloves!*" As a matter of fact, such a recuperation of our losses was inconceivable at that time. The play seemed anti-Communist because the audience was on Hugo's side. Hoederer's murder was taken as an equivalent of the crimes imputed to the Kominform. Above all, the Machiavellian plotting of the leaders in the play and their reversal of policy at the end was a condemnation of the Communist Party in the eyes of its adversaries. Politically, that was the most

truthful moment in the play: in Communist Parties everywhere in
the world, when an opposition group attempts to introduce a new
and correct line of policy, it is liquidated (with or without physical
violence ; then the leaders take the new policy and use it for their
own purposes. In the case of Illyria—inspired by Hungary—the
Party's hesitations and its final decision were justified by the circumstances; it was simply that its internal difficulties were exposed to
people who were looking at it from outside with animosity. They
gave the play a meaning which it did, in fact, have for them. It was
for this reason that Sartre refused several times to let it be acted in
other countries.

In October, a great many Vichyists had rallied to the R.P.F. and
a great many collaborators were getting back up on their perches.
Flandin was writing in *L'Aurore,* Montherlant was having *Le Maître
de Santiago* put on, and Sacha Guitry was doing his *Diable Boiteux,*
a transparent apology for the collaboration. Maurras was preparing a
lawsuit against Stéphane and Bourdet. Under Mauriac's wing, *La
Table Ronde* fraternally opened its pages to ex-collaborators and
their friends. (Camus made the mistake of writing for the first issue,
but then realized his error and didn't repeat it.) A spate of books
appeared excusing or justifying the policies of Pétain, a thing which
would have been inconceivable two years earlier; in his *Lettre à
Mauriac,* Bardèche went so far as to defend *Je Suis Partout.* Boutang
was giving lectures for the greater glory of Maurras. Pétain's name
was cheered in meetings, and in April a "Committee for the Liberation of Pétain" was formed. In certain circles, people talked sar-
castically about "the Resistentialists," and spoke of the Resistance as
though it had been a fashion, intended to serve the personal interests
of its followers. A counterpurge swept the country; ex-Resistance
members were accused of performing summary executions, were ar-
raigned and often condemned.

I was moving somewhat in theatrical circles, because of Sartre,
and often heard things that appalled me. It was said that Jean Ri-
gaud, running through a list of well-known people in the audience
before he went on, had come across some Jewish names and mur-
mured: "They must have put them in incubators, not crematoria."
This witticism was retailed with appreciative laughter. At the Véfour, the person sitting next to me, pretending not to be able to read
the menu I was holding, asked: "What's that? Cutlets à la Buchenwald?" I didn't want to make a scene and I said to myself: "After all,

it's only words." But the fact that people dared say them meant something. Yesterday's profiteers assumed the role of victims and explained how base it was to be on the side of the conquerors. They pitied poor Brinon; they turned Brasillach into a gentle martyr. I rejected all such betrayals; I had my own martyrs. When I thought of them and told myself that so much grief and misery had been in vain, I was filled with distress. Behind us, that great cadaver, the War, was finally decomposing, and the air was sickening with the stench.

Now that rehearsals were finished, there was nothing to keep us in Paris and we went to the South of France. I chose Ramatuelle, where we found a country inn which had rooms with red tile floors; the dining room was a glass enclosure opening onto a garden and then beyond, far off, the sea. In the evening a wood fire glowed on the hearth; every morning, I worked in the sunshine, under the flowering trees. We were the only ones there; it was almost as if it were our own house. We went up to the Saracen towers, and down to Saint-Tropez to have a drink at the harbor or buy Provençal skirts at Vachon's. I worked, and I read Henry du Moulin de Labarthète's memoirs about Vichy and Gide's correspondence with Jammes.

Bost, who had rented a little house at Cabris with Olga, came over and spent two days with us. He was there at lunchtime one day when Simone Berriau, wearing her hooded cape and followed by her husband, Brandel, and Yves Mirande, sprang out of an American car. They had all come from Mauvannes, the property she owned near Hyères. She came into the dining room and trumpeted in her grand manner, with a gesture toward her husband: "Do you know what this gentleman did to me this morning?" Then she told us. "All right," said Mirande, "but there's no need to tell the servants about it." We spent a day and a night at Mauvannes; in the morning, when she was alone with me on the terrace, Simone gave me the benefit of confidences so precise, and so abundantly accompanied by winks of complicity, that I wanted the ground to open up and swallow me. She loved to play at matchmaking and found it impossible to conceive that a young actress should refuse to jump into bed with the first millionaire who presented himself. She had great vitality and persistence, but they were exclusively at the service of her own interests. Yet she seemed to be sincerely attached to Mirande, who lived in her house. He was an outmoded embodiment of the *esprit boulevardier* so dear to my father and, despite his age, still obsessed with the fair sex; his conversation was highly spiced but funny; he had a *"fleur bleue"* side to him, and that always sits well on rakes. He told us that in Hollywood he had had a passionate liaison with Greta Garbo; though heartbroken, he had broken it off: "Because I didn't want to make myself ridiculous," he said, adding what seemed to me a mysterious comment, coming from his lips: "And besides, she had vices." He was charming with Sartre. His witticisms, his laughter and his kindness lightened the burden of many meetings that the presence of Simone Berriau's husband did nothing to enliven.

Sartre was getting very gloomy letters from M.; she had reluctantly agreed to spend four months with him while I was on my trip with Algren. A few days before I was due to leave, she wrote to Sartre saying that she had decided not to see him again, on those conditions. This threw me into a great perplexity. I wanted enormously to be back with Algren, but after all I had only lived with him for three weeks; I didn't really know how much he meant to me: a little, a lot, or even more? The question would have been an idle one if circumstances had decided for me; but suddenly I had a choice: Knowing I could have stayed with Sartre, I was leaving myself open to regrets which might turn into a grudge against Algren, or at least into bitterness against myself. I opted for half measures: two months of America instead of four. Algren was expecting me to stay a long time, and I didn't dare announce my new arrangements in black and white; I would talk things over with him when I got there.

This time I took a plane that flew high and fast. It landed me at two in the morning in Iceland, where I drank coffee surrounded by bearded old sea dogs; when we took off again I was dazzled by the landscape: a silvery light on high white mountains at the edge of a smooth sea, against a raspberry-colored sky. I flew over snow-covered Labrador and landed at La Guardia. My visa gave the purpose of my trip as "lectures." "On what?" the immigration official on duty asked me; when I said philosophy he shuddered. "What philosophy?" He allowed me five minutes in which to give him a brief account. I said it was impossible. "Has it got anything to do with politics? Are you a Communist? You wouldn't admit it if you were." I got the impression that any French person was suspect *a priori*. After having consulted some files he gave me an authorization to stay for three weeks.

I spent the day with Fernand and Stépha; it was raining in torrents and I was in limbo. New York seemed less opulent than the year before because Paris no longer looked so impoverished; except in the very elegant bars, the over-long skirts of the New Look made the women look like scullery maids. The next day, under a scorching sun, New York along the East River seemed like a great Mediterranean port. I looked up some of my friends and went to see *The Respectful Prostitute:* a disaster! Most of the scenes between Lizzie and the Negro had been cut, and they talked in flat voices without even looking at one another. All the same, they had reached their hundredth performance and the house was full.

The day after that, at midnight, I landed in Chicago and spent the next twenty-four hours wondering what I was doing there. Algren took me in the afternoon to visit a gang of junky thieves whom I simply *had* to visit, according to him. I spent two hours in a filthy den, surrounded by strangers talking, too fast for me to follow, to other strangers. There was a forty-year-old woman, an habitual offender drugged to her eyeballs; her ex-husband, with an enormous pallid face, even farther gone than she was, who spent his nights playing drums to earn some money and his days at the wheel of a taxi, driving round the city looking for fixes; also her present lover, wanted by the police for theft and fraud. They all lived together. The woman had a ravishing daughter, respectably married two months ago, who was there visiting. For her sake, the trio made an effort to appear decent. All the same, the ex-husband rushed into the bathroom and gave himself a shot under Algren's nose—they were trying in vain to draw him into their rites. All they really enjoyed was to be with other addicts and chat about syringes, Algren told me. My anxiety was quickly dissipated when I found myself alone with him again. The next day I went with him to see the wife of a thief, also in hiding from the police, who had started to write since he had known Algren; she was waiting in tears for her husband, but she displayed with great pride the book he had written and which he had had typed at his own expense; she was raising two deaf-mute children. Meanwhile we were going about in the rain, shopping and making arrangements. The Guatemalan official who gave me my visa spent an hour explaining how much his country loved France. He was very curt with Algren, especially when Algren stated his nationality: "American citizen." "Citizen of the United States," the official corrected him. "We are both Americans."

After a day of phlegmatic but frantic agitation, we took the morning train for Cincinnati: 700,000 inhabitants; squares, green hills, birds, provincial calm. We ate dinner watching television, which was beginning to appear in all public places. The evening of the following day we embarked on a side-wheeler. It was a holiday in Cincinnati. Airplanes and searchlights were wheeling around the sky, there were bonfires along both banks of the river, and the headlights of the automobiles lit up the great metal bridges; then we slid off into the darkness and silence of the country.

I loved the monotony of the voyage through this wide watery landscape. On deck, in the sun, I translated one of Algren's stories, I read, and we chatted over glasses of Scotch; Algren kept trying to take photographs with a German camera he didn't understand; he was quite satisfied because he had managed to get a tiny noise out of it when he pressed down a catch. In the evening light, I saw the waters of the Ohio mingle with those of the Mississippi. I had dreamed of the Mississippi listening to "Old Man River," and also while I was writing *All Men Are Mortal*. But I could never have imagined the enchantment of its evenings, its moons.

Each day we went ashore for a few hours. Louisville, sinister in the rain; a little town in Kentucky with decrepit bars full of celebrating farmers; Memphis—cotton bales along the docks, cotton factories, cotton brokers' offices; Natchez, one of the oldest towns in the South, with 40,000 inhabitants. The landing jetty turned out to be at the very end of the town. A huge man came up and offered to drive us downtown by car. Despite the heaviness of the heat, like most whites he was wearing a stiff collar and a suit. He explained to us that in Natchez the Negroes led an extremely easy life, and took great care to avoid calling them niggers; he only let the word slip out once. We left him at the edge of the Negro quarter. We went out by taxi to look at the old plantations, among others that of Jefferson Davis. We drew up in front of an extravagant, columned house whose construction had been interrupted by the Civil War and which was decaying among giant trees draped with Spanish moss. An old woman made a fuss because Algren wanted to take a photograph. The chauffeur shrugged his shoulders. "That's the owner's sister; *she's from New York*," he said with distaste. Here the whites and the blacks understand one another, he explained, because both groups stay in their place. The Negroes are polite. But in California, he said with sudden rage, they don't take off their hats, they say just "Yes" and "No," and they talk to the whites! He was nervous, furious at having to serve as a guide to people from the North. That evening we passed Baton Rouge. Behind the lights of the port and the illuminated buildings, the tall furnaces were spitting out flames. The afternoon of the following day we landed at New Orleans.

In the heart of the French Quarter, we found an immense room, with a huge electric fan and a wooden balcony overlooking a patio. There were burlesque dancers and young prostitutes wandering around the hotel corridors in housecoats, and the owner, a fat, half-mad Russian woman obstinately decreed that I too was Russian. After a creole dinner and ices *flambés au rhum,* we went out to look for the Napoleon Bar at the Absinthe House, for julep zombies and some good jazz; but it appeared that there was no longer any Negro jazz in the white quarter. Spring was already over; the azaleas were gone and the rains had stopped, the weather was heavy and dry. We spent the day swimming in Lake Pontchartrain. None of Algren's photographs had come out.

Next came Yucatán, with its jungle, its fields of blue aloes, its red flamboyant trees; Mérida, its Spanish churches amid subtropical damp and luxuriance. I have already described our trip to Chichén-Itzá in *The Mandarins.* The ruins of Uxmal were even more beautiful, but to see them one had to catch a bus at six in the morning and we couldn't even find anywhere to have a cup of coffee. Algren, overcome with despair in the presence of these stubborn stones, refused to give them so much as a glance; I explored them all on my own with a far from light heart. These sullen moods were rare; he accepted everything, the beans, the tortillas, the insects, the heat, captivated as I was by the little Indian girls with their long skirts and shiny braids, and exactly the same features we saw on the bas-reliefs in the Mayan temples. I have already described what we liked in Guatemala. But the streets were sad: the women went barefoot, dressed in magnificent, filthy materials; the men trotted along, crushed beneath their heavy burdens. In front of the wooden or mud huts thatched with straw which clustered together to form hamlets were children with swollen bellies and eyes blinded by trachoma. The Indians, 67 percent of the population, had been free for only twelve years; before 1936, on the pretext that they were repaying debts, they were kept in penal servitude; when we saw them they were living just as they had then, in wretched and hopeless poverty, and it seemed to me that they submitted to it with a stupefied inertia.

Mexico City was a real town where things were happening; we wandered around in the residential quarters and in the districts of dubious reputation. One evening we let ourselves be persuaded into

attending a show of "native dancing" actually organized by an old
American con man; it consisted of tourists long past the bloom of
youth soulfully applauding as young women in luxurious costumes
went through imitations of peasant dances. We walked out after half
an hour and by way of revenge ended up in the sleaziest joint in the
entire slum area; here enormous taxi-girls were dancing with tiny
evil-looking Mexicans, Indians and Spaniards; we were stared at with
surprise, and some of them came over to talk to us while we were
emptying our glasses of tequila. For most Americans, Mexico City is
a jungle with an assassin working full time on every street corner.
But Algren had been around hundreds of cutthroats in his life without seeing a single throat cut. And in any case, he told me, the
incidence of crimes is much lower in Mexico City than it is in New
York or Chicago. On Sunday we went to see the bullfights in the
giant arenas; out of a dozen, there were three or four really good
ones. What annoyed Algren was that each *corrida* constituted a self-
terminating event, whereas a boxer's victory opens a fresh cycle of
challenges and bouts. On the way out we mingled with the crowd
and followed it a long way into the outlying districts; we came back
to the center of town to eat turkey with chocolate sauce, tamales
which practically burned away one's mouth, and murderous *chili con
carne*. At night it rained and in the morning we would walk through
big puddles under the mildest of blue skies.

I hadn't yet broached the subject of my departure, not having the
heart to do it as soon as I arrived; the following weeks I still couldn't
face it. Every day it became more urgent and more difficult. During a
long bus journey between Mexico City and Morelia, I announced to
Algren with clumsy flippancy that I would have to be back in Paris
on the 14th of July. "Oh, all right," he said. I'm flabbergasted today
when I look back and think how I allowed myself to be fooled by his
indifference. At Morelia, I found it quite natural that he shouldn't
want to get out and walk around; I strolled gaily through the streets
and squares of the old Spanish town on my own. Gaily, I visited the
market of Pazcuaro where Indians dressed in blue sold blue fabrics.
We went across the lake to the island of Janitzio, decorated from top
to bottom with fishermen's nets; I bought some embroidered blouses.
We walked back from the jetty to the hotel and I began making
plans for the next day. Algren stopped me; he'd had enough of Indians and markets, of Mexico, and of traveling. I thought it was just
another fit of temper like the one at Uxmal and not of any particular

consequence. All the same, it lasted a long time and I began to get uneasy. He walked on in front of me, very fast; when I caught up with him, he wouldn't talk to me. At the hotel I went on plying him with questions: "What's the matter? Everything was going so well; why are you spoiling everything?" Far from being moved by my distress, which eventually reduced me to tears, he just walked out on me. When he came back we were reconciled, though without explanations; that was enough to restore my equanimity. The next few days I was quite carefree. We saw Cholula with its three hundred churches; at Puebla, whose brothel district reminded me of the Rue Bouterie, the little prostitutes deloused their children on the thresholds of their rooms, all open to the passers-by. Enormous dark green trees shaded the old colonial squares of Cuernavaca. At Taxco, sprawling over hills, in the heart of the silver mines, they sold silver jewelry along the streets; we drank delicious whiskey sours on the terrace of a hotel, surrounded by bougainvilleas and overlooking a beautiful baroque church. "At the end of two days I'd be shooting off a revolver in the streets just to make something happen," Algren said; Mexico was decidedly getting on his nerves. All right. We took a plane to New York.

In the white-hot streets, women walked about under vast cocktail hats, their bosoms exposed almost down to the nipples and their navels bare; the city had taken on carnival colors, while remaining hard and bustling. I began to pay for my cowardice and my thoughtlessness. Algren didn't talk to me in quite the same way he used to, and every now and then I even felt a stab of hostility from him. One evening I asked him: "Don't you care for me as much as you did?" "No," he said, "it's not the same anymore." I cried all night, leaning out of the window between the silence of the sky and the city's indifferent noises. We were living in the Brittany on lower Fifth Avenue; we wandered around the Village; I dragged myself along over the hot asphalt; we bought bricks of black raspberry ice cream and ate them in our room; my throat still burned. We spent painful hours in French restaurants on the East Side, where I dragged him in search of a little respite from the heat, and in the suffocating West Side restaurants which he preferred because they didn't oblige him to wear a jacket and tie. It was my turn to resent him on account of his sullen behavior. One evening, when we had dined in a tavern in the open air in the middle of Central Park and then went on to listen to jazz at Café Society, he was particularly disagreeable. "I can leave tomorrow," I told him; we exchanged a few more words and then suddenly he said to me impulsively: "I'm ready to marry you this very moment." I realized I would never be able to harbor rancor in my heart against him for anything ever again; all the wrongs were on my side. I left him on the 14th of July, uncertain whether I would ever see him again. What a nightmare, that return flight, high over the ocean, plunged into a night without beginning and without end, stuffing myself with sleeping pills, unable to sleep, lost, and utterly dismayed!

If I had the honesty and the intelligence to let Algren know the limits of my stay before going over to see him, things would have worked out better; doubtless he'd have received me with less ardor, but would have had no reason to feel bitter toward me. I've often wondered what part his sudden disappointment actually played in our affair. I think it did nothing more, in fact, than disclose to him a situation he wouldn't have accepted for long in any case. At first sight, it was identical with mine. Even if Sartre hadn't existed, I would never have gone to live permanently in Chicago; or if I had tried to do so, I would certainly not have been able to bear more than one or two years of an exile which would have destroyed both my reasons for writing and the possibility of doing so. On his side, although I often suggested it to him, Algren could never have come to live in Paris, even for six months of the year; to write, he needed to stay rooted in his own country, in his own city, in the world he had created for himself. We had both already shaped our lives, and there could be no question of transplanting them elsewhere. Yet our feelings were, for both of us, far more than a diversion or even an escape; each of us regretted bitterly that the other refused to come and live with him.

But there was one great difference between us. I spoke his native language, I also knew the literature and history of his country pretty well, I read the books he loved and the books he wrote; when I was near him I forgot myself, I entered his world. He knew almost nothing about mine; he had read a few articles I had written, scarcely any more of Sartre's work, and French writers in general held little interest for him. Also, I was far better off in Paris than he was in Chicago; he was a prey to the harsh loneliness of America. Now that I existed, the emptiness around him became indistinguishable from my absence, and he blamed me for it. Our farewells tore at my heart, too; but primarily because Algren let me leave with the uncertainty